B"H

BAAL SHEM TOV

RABBI YISRAEL BEN ELIEZER
THE LEGENDARY KABBALAH MASTER

GENESIS EXODUS

MYSTICAL TEACHINGS ON
THE WEEKLY TORAH PORTION

VOLUME I

By **Rabbi Doctor Eliezer Shore**

BST Publishing
Cleveland, Ohio

Translation and Commentary by Rabbi Doctor Eliezer Shore
Copyright© 2012 by BST Publishing
Printed in the United States of America

All rights reserved. Permission is granted to copy or reprint portions of this book for any noncommercial use, except they may not be posted on line without permission, except for the inclusion of brief quotations for a review.

For information regarding permission to reprint material from this book, please e-mail your request to info@bstpublishing.com

ISBN: 978-0-9853562-2-4

Library of Congress Control Number: 2012943012
Library of Congress subject heading:
1. Hasidim — Legends. 2. Baal Shem Tov, ca. 1700—1760 — Legends. 3. Hasidism. 4. Mysticism Judaism. 5. Title.

BST Publishing
Cleveland, OH 44124
info@bstpublishing.com

www.bstpublishing.com

Dedicated to the millions of Chassidim and their Rebbes, who for nearly three centuries, have cherished and passed these holy stories down to us.

יברכך יי וישמרך
יאר יי פניו אליך ויחנך
ישא יי פניו אליך וישם לך שלום

"May the L•rd bless you and guard you. May the L•rd make His countenance shine upon you and be gracious to you. May the L•rd turn His countenance towards you and grant you peace."

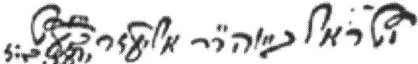

Yisrael Ben Moreinu Rabbeinu HaRav Rav Eliezer KoesB (presently in) Medzibush
Signature of the Baal Shem Tov

TABLE OF CONTENTS

PREFACE 7

CHAPTER ONE [BEREISHIT].............................. 11
CHAPTER TWO [NOACH] 19
CHAPTER THREE [LECH LECHA] 23
CHAPTER FOUR [VAYEIRA] 31
CHAPTER FIVE [CHAYA SARAH]........................ 35
CHAPTER SIX [TOLDOT]..................................... 41
CHAPTER SEVEN [VAYEITZEI] 59
CHAPTER EIGHT [VAYISHLACH] 69
CHAPTER NINE [VAYESHEV].............................. 81
CHAPTER TEN [MIKETZ] 91
CHAPTER 11 [VAYIGASH]................................. 101
CHAPTER 12 [VAYECHI] 105
CHAPTER 13 [SHEMOT] 109
CHAPTER 14 [VAYERA] 121
CHAPTER 15 [BO].. 131
CHAPTER 16 [BESHALACH] 139
CHAPTER 17 [YISRO].. 149
CHAPTER 18 [MISHPATIM] 159

CHAPTER 19 [TERUMAH].................................167
CHAPTER 20 [TETZAVAH].................................173
CHAPTER 21 [KI TETZAH].................................177
CHAPTER 22 [VAYAKHEL].................................183
CHAPTER 23 [PEKUDEI] 189

APPENDIX...195
GLOSSARY..197
BIBLIOGRAPHY..203

PREFACE

Into the terrifying, lightless night that marked Jewish life in seventeenth and eighteenth century Eastern Europe, Heaven sent Rabbi Yisrael ben Eliezer, known as the Baal Shem Tov. His purpose was to lead, guide and inspire the masses of ordinary, unlearned Jewish people (the vast majority) of their immense, spiritual value and of the importance of their living according to the ancient ways of the Jewish faith. He accomplished his mission by founding the Chassidic movement and spreading the new teachings of Chassidism.

The basis of Chassidic thought derives from the powerful spirit of the Baal Shem Tov probing the mystical aspects of the Torah. The most fundamental teaching of Chassidism is the omnipresence of G•d, that is, the whole universe is a manifestation of the Divine. This manifestation is not an "Emanation" but an actual "Portion" of G•d; nothing is separate from G•d. Therefore, everything in creation, including man, animals, plants and even inanimate objects are directly, and at all times supervised by G•d.

Characterized by an extraordinary sincerity and simplicity, the Baal Shem Tov spoke directly to the masses of unlearned Jews. His teachings, called Chassidus, emphasized each person's continuous spiritual union with G•d, and that enthusiasm and joy are essential to be in an experiential relationship with Him. He taught that religious life consisted not only of religious scholarship, but also of a sincere love of G•d combined with warm faith and belief in the effectiveness of prayer; that the ordinary person filled with a sincere belief in G•d, and whose prayers come from the heart, is more acceptable to G•d than someone versed in and fully observant of Jewish law but lacking inspiration in their divine service.

Chassidus was cherished and loved by the common and often illiterate Jews. Among them, it found its home. Chassidic sayings of wisdom and stories and anecdotes about the Rebbes, the leaders of the various Chassidic Courts, became part of a vibrant Jewish life that thrives on even today.

The beit midrash (study hall) of the holy Baal Shem Tov served as a synagogue and as a place to gather and learn Torah. Moreover, it became a

PREFACE

spiritual center that drew his followers and even non-believers to ask advice from Rebbe, the Baal Shem Tov, and to receive blessings about their personal lives.

The Baal Shem instilled his very spirit into his inner circle of followers, known as the "Chevraya Kadisha," the Holy Fellowship. His teachings struck a responsive chord in their hearts, and they eagerly undertook to follow his way of worship and thought. The inner circle of devout followers saw in the Baal Shem Tov the image of the ancient ideal, the Torah master who embodied the power of King David and the spiritual countenance like an angel of G•d. They considered it a rare privilege to be able to spend time in the atmosphere of the Rebbe's great holiness.

Those of the inner circle, who studied within the walls of the Baal Shem Tov's beth midrash were the "first sources" who absorbed the teachings and miraculous accounts about their Rebbe.

The present collection of teachings were published as a collection in Sefer Baal Shem Tov, were written by those closest to the Baal Shem Tov, and therefore are considered factual accounts of his extraordinary teachings about the depths of the Torah.

CHAPTER ONE

BEREISHIT

GENESIS

"In the beginning . . . ." *Genesis 1:1*

1.1 When the Moshiach comes, may it be speedily in our days, he will expound upon the letter combinations of each word of the Torah, from beginning to end.[1] Then he will join the entire Torah into one word,[2] so that the letter

---

[1] The letters of the Torah, though inscribed in a pattern that tells the story of the creation of the world, and the history and laws of the Jewish people, are not fixed. It is possible to rearrange the letters to gain new insights into the meaning of the text, and G•d's will for man. Furthermore, the letters of Torah represent the creative energies of G•d that enter the world, and arranging them in different patterns can affect the flow of energy from above. By meditating on the letters in their different combinations, mystical states of consciousness can be obtained. There are various techniques for letter combination, such as *tzerufi osiot* (letter recombination); *gematria* (using the numerical value of each Hebrew letter), *roshei tevos* and *sofei tevos* (words derived from the first and last letters of words in a verse); and the division of letters into their component parts. Thus, there is an infinite amount of meaning that can be derived from the Torah.

[2] See *Zohar 3*: "The Torah is all one holy Name of the Holy One." Also, ibid. 2:90b: "The Torah is really all one Name of G•d. Fortunate is the lot of one who merits it. One who merits the Torah, merits the holy Name." See also ibid. 3:73a, 3:268b, 2:144a. See, also, *Bris Menucha*, Introduction, p. 3c: "About this, they said that

BEREISHIT

permutations will be without number. Then he will expound upon all the combinations.

Teshuos Chen, Tazria

1.2 The Talmud states about the Ten Utterances of Creation,[3] that the word *"Bereishit"* is also an utterance. Why then does the Torah not use the words "And He said?"[4]

This is because the brilliance of that first utterance is too great to perceive.[5]

Kisvei Kodesh, p. 26a

---

the entire Torah is all one Name, and all the words are Names that can cause effects."

[3] The opening chapter of Genesis contains nine verses that state: "And G•d said . . . . ." Yet, the Talmud calls these the "Ten Utterances." (*Megilah 21b*)

[4] I.e. "And G•d said, Beginning!"

[5] Rabbi Tzvi Elimelech Shapira of Dinov (*Bnei Yisaschar, Chodesh Kislev — Teves* 4:49) explained that each of the Divine Utterances used in creating the world were actually channels that funneled the Divine light into creation. In the same way as human speech both limits the flow of thought at the same time as it reveals it, so these Utterances limit G•d's infinite light in the process of revealing the creation. These channels are the letters and words through which G•d creates. The word *Bereishit* refers to a level *before* the creation of letters. It is the world in G•d's mind, as it were, before the contraction of His light into letters and channels. Thus it transcends all means of perception. According to R. Shapira, this is alluded to in the verse itself: "In the

GENESIS

"In the beginning . . . . ." *Genesis 1:1*

1.3 And the faithfulness of your times shall be a stock of salvation, wisdom and knowledge, and the fear of G•d is His storehouse. (*Isaiah 33:6*). "Faithfulfulness" is the Mishnaic Order of *Zeraim*.[6] "Your times" is *Mo'ed*. "Stock" is *Nashim*. "Salvation" is *Nezikim*. "Wisdom" is *Kodshim*. "Knowledge" is *Tahoros*. Nevertheless, "the fear of G•d is his storehouse."[7]

This is like a man who said to his worker, "Put a bushel of wheat in the loft for me." After the worker went and did it he asked the worker, "Did you mix in a handful of salt,"[8]. "No," the worker

---

beginning, G•d created..." "*Bereishit bara es . . . .*" The . . *es* (את) alludes to the entire Hebrew alphabet. The verse implies that "In the beginning, G•d first created the letters from *aleph* to *tav*, ת — א." The word *Bereishit*, however, precedes the creation of the letters.

[6] The Mishnah is constituted of six major sections: *Zeraim* — Acrigultural laws; *Mo'ed* — Seasons; *Nashim* — Marital Relations (lit. "Women"); *Nezikin* — Damages; *Kodshim* — the Sacrificial Order; *Taharos* — Ritual Purity. The Talmud finds an allusion to each of these sections in the verse from Isaiah.

[7] Meaning, this is the main thing, as the Talmud explains with a parable.

[8] To prevent it from becoming bug infested.

replied. "Then it would have been better had you never put it up there," the man said.

My grandfather [the Baal Shem Tov] pointed out a discrepancy in this parable. According to the parable, the salt is secondary to the wheat, which is the main thing. However, in the [Talmud's interpretation of the] verse, the fear of G•d is the main thing, while the Torah is secondary.

With pure words, he gave a great answer. His mouth spoke mighty things of the innermost hidden secrets. The essence of what he said is as follows. When the Holy One created the world, it was unable to exist, for everything kept returning to its source in the Infinite. But when He finally created Israel, the world could exist. Now, the name Israel, ישראל, alludes to this. The *reish* is *Chochma*, the *lamed* is *Binah*, and the *aleph* is *Da'at*, and the remaining letters, *yud — shin*, is the substance (*yesh* — יש) through which the world exists, making it something from nothing.[9] This is Israel, and the existence of all the worlds that were created *ex nihilo*. Therefore, Israel sustains all the worlds and the creation, for if they did not, everything would return to its original state of nothingness. It is the existence of Israel that maintains all the worlds.

---

[9] *Yesh m'ayin* — יש מאין.

However, this is only when a Jew has no more existence than is necessary to maintain the world, as opposed to when he has too much, G•d forbid.[10]

This is the essence of his awesome words. The mouth cannot express all that is implied by them. Words would be exhausted by their great depth and our limited understanding. To my mind, they allude to the entire Torah.

Degel Machane Ephraim, Veschanan

"In the beginning, G•d created the world . . . . ."
Genesis 1:1

1.4 It was impossible to create the world, for it would have expanded infinitely. Therefore, G•d looked at the deeds of the wicked,[11] and greatly

---

[10] The Hebrew word *yesh* means "existence" or "substance" — both material and spiritual. An overabundance of *yeshus* (pl.) means having more ego and a sense of self than is necessary.

[11] The Midrash states that before the creation, G•d foresaw the deeds of the righteous, and created the world on their account. However, the world that G•d desired to create on their account was overflowing with love for them. As such, it was unable to exist in the Divine Effulgence. G•d therefore looked at the deeds of the wicked, which resulted in a withholding of His light. But it was precisely this withholding that allows the

BEREISHIT

contracted His light.[12] Then he looked at the deeds of the righteous and drew down a line of life, in the mystery of "below and not below."

All of this is known from the writings of our Master, the Arizal, and the Light of Israel, the Baal Shem Tov.

Heichal HaBracha, Bereishit

1.5 When it arose in the will of the Blessed One to bestow upon the creation, that is, when He beheld the deeds of the righteous, there was an arousal of his Will, and a great longing to bestow upon them. Because of this, it arose in His mind to create the world. However, the great outpouring of love would have completely annulled the creation, and it therefore had to be held back. That is, G•d looked at the deeds of the wicked and *Gevuros* were aroused in the world.[13] This made it possible to create the world.[14]   *Teshuos Chen, Chayah Sarah*

---

world to exist. There is a constant pendulum movement, between the desire to create and the desire to restrain. This is known as "below and not below" — מטי ולא מטי.

[12] According to the teachings of the Arizal, the first stage in creation was the *tzimzum,* the contraction of G•d's light to make room for the existence of a finite universe.

[13] *Gevurah* (pl. *Gevuros*) means "strength" or "power," and refers to the forces of contraction and restraint that G•d used in creating the world. (As the Mishna says in

GENESIS

Pirkei Avos 4:1: "Who is strong? One who subdues his own nature.")

[14] Implied in both this teaching and the previous one is that deeds of the wicked also contain a point of goodness, since they provide the context in which G•d could create the world. This reflects the Baal Shem Tov's teaching that there is a spark of holiness in all things, and that light shines greater when it comes out of darkness.

CHAPTER TWO

NOACH

GENESIS

"These are the descendants of Noach: Noach was a righteous man, faultless in his generation . . . ." *Noach 6:9*

2.1 A person is called a Tzaddik — in the mystery of "A Tzaddik is the foundation of the world." *Proverbs 10:25* — when he takes great pleasure in serving G•d, for "From my flesh, I will behold G•d." *Job 19:26.*[15]

Toldot Yaakov Yosef, Va'eschanan, p. 179b

2.2 "From my flesh, I will behold G•d." Just as sexual intercourse cannot result in birth unless the male organ is vibrant and full of desire and joy, so to spiritual union, through words of Torah and prayer, can only give birth if it is with a vibrant

---

[15] Chasidic writings cite this verse often to support the idea that the physical, emotional and mental constituents of a human being parallel and reflect the workings of the supernal Sefiros through which G•d directs the world. From our physicality, we can understand how the divine superstructure of creation functions. The Sefirah of Yesod, (literally "Foundation") corresponds in the human dimension to the phallus. And just as this organ is the focus of physical pleasure, so a Tzaddik, who is the "foundation" of the world, takes intense spiritual pleasure in serving G•d. This pleasure is itself a rarified and uplifted expression of sexual pleasure.

NOACH

organ,[16] and with joy and pleasure. Thus, a person who studies Torah and serves G•d for the sake of Heaven, to give satisfaction to G•d without receiving any reward, merits to taste sweetness, pleasantness and delight in the Torah and Divine service. Then, he gives birth spiritually, just like physical union when done with pleasure and joy. But when a person studies Torah and serves G•d not for the sake of Heaven, this is not the case. He has no pleasure and delight, and does not give birth.

Ben Poras Yosef, Noach, p. 19d

2.3 I heard from my Master, that when someone asked Nachmanidies, "What is considered the service of G•d?" he answered, "Whatever has delight and joy, combined with fear."

Toldot Yaakov Yosef, Mishpatim, p. 70b

2.4 In the material world, where there is fear, there is no joy, and where there is joy, there is no fear. However, in the service of G•d, where there is fear

---

[16] Meaning, the entire person must be in a state of joy and ecstasy during prayer.

there is love. Afterward, I found this in the work of Algazi.[17]

Toldot Yaakov Yosef, Bechukosai, p. 127b

2.5 Serve G•d with fear and joy — these are two friends that are never apart. For fear without joy is depression, and it is wrong to suffer over how to serve G•d, just always be happy. For even then, you must serve Him, and there is no time to consider how or what.

Tzivos HaRivash 13b

---

[17] Either Israel Jacob Algazi (1680 — 1756) or Yom Tov Algazi (1727 — 1802). Both were Kabbalists and Halachists.

CHAPTER THREE

LECH LECHA

GENESIS

"And G•d said to Abram, 'Go out from your land, from your birthplace, and from your father's house, to the land that I will show you.'" Lech Lecha 12:1

"I will make your nature known in the world."

Rashi

3.1 I heard from my Master in the name of Rav Sa'adiah Gaon, that a person is created in this world solely to break his negative, inborn character traits. Through this, he raises up the level called "your nature [i.e., what is natural for you] in the world" — [i.e., into the world] Above." It is called "world" (*olam*) from the word "hidden" (*he'elam*) and "concealed."

Kesser Shem Tov, p. 3b

3.2 For instance, if the heat of his liver causes him to be hot tempered,[18] he should break his nature and his anger as much as possible. Likewise, if an over excitable nature causes him to spill seed, G•d forbid, he should break this [characteristic]. And one who is depressed by nature, who bemoans and

---

[18] Anger was thought to be a result of too much heat in the liver.

LECH LECHA

complains even when serving G•d, has no virtue. And if his nature is to be a hedonist and reveler, he should break his nature and do the opposite.

This is what the Sages said: "One who is born on a Tuesday will be wealthy and adulterous (*atir v'zanai*)."[19] The problem is that these are opposite traits. If he is adulterous, it is more likely that he will be poor, as it is written: "On account of a harlot, a man is brought to a loaf of bread . . . . ." (*Proverbs 6:26*).[20] "He with big pumpkins and she with small ones."[21]

Rather, this must refer to a person who by nature is adulterous, but who breaks his nature and becomes a *zanai* — one who sells different

---

[19] *Shabbat 156a*.
[20] See *Sotah* ... "Whoever has relations with a harlot will ... a loaf of bread.'"
[21] *Megilah 1* ... Scroll of Esther states: "On t... heart of the king was merry w... to bring Vashti the queen b... al crown, to show the people a... princes her beauty; for she was fair to look upo... (Esther 1,10,11). The Gemara comments that just as King Achashverus had ... entious intent, so was Queen Vashti willing to appear for the same reason. "He with big pumpkins and she with small ones" — i.e. both their intentions were for evil. However, it is not clear how this proves the Baal Shem Tov's point that promiscuity leads to poverty.

types of foodstuff (*mazon*), as Rashi says about Rachav: "A woman of *zonah*" (*Joshua 2:1*) — that she sold different types of *mazon*. Therefore, it is good that he is rich and a *zanai*.

Ben Poras Yosef, p. 85b

". . . . . and all the families of the earth will bless (their children to be like) you." *Lech Lecha 12:3*

3.3 When there are a number of wicked people in a city or in a country who act deceitfully, and there is one Tzaddik among them who acts truthfully, when he studies Torah, prays and attaches himself to truth, "all the workers of iniquity and liars will be dispersed."[22]

Toldot Yaakov Yosef, Vayera, p. 20c

"And Abram took Sarai, his wife, and Lot, his bother's son, and all the possessions they had acquired, and the people they had (converted) in

---

[22] From *Psalms 92:10*. See *Imrei Peninim, p. 209a* for a similar teaching in which the Baal Shem Tov seems to be referring to community leaders who act deceitfully and arrogantly.

LECH LECHA

Haran; and they left to go into the land of Canaan . . . . ." *Lech Lecha 12:5*

3.4 When a person is in a state of small mindedness (*mohin d'katnus*), he gives birth to the souls of converts.[23] This is the meaning of: "the

---

[23] This idea, found throughout the teachings of the Baal Shem Tov, is based upon the principle of root and branch souls. When a root soul falls to a lower level, it is in order to raise up the "branch" souls that are connected to it, who themselves are on a low level. Although converts may have very high souls according to the Talmud, they observe the mitzvos with more exactitude than born Jews before their conversion, their souls are locked in a Gentile body. A similar teaching can be found in the writings of the Baal Shem Tov concerning *ba'alei teshuva* — returnees to Judaism. Their ability to repent comes from the influence of a Tzaddik who has fallen to a lower level and raised himself again.

See *Kedushas Levi*, by R. Levi Yitzchak of Berditchev, on the verse: "Your ointments have a goodly fragrance." *(Song of Songs 1:3)* "It is necessary to understand why G•d created a situation in which a Tzaddik falls from his level. It would certainly be better for him to remain constantly on his level and serve G•d with an expanded consciousness and to love Him perfectly. The Baal Shem Tov and my Master, Rabbi Dov Baer (the Maggid of Mezritch) explained it as follows. When the Tzaddik falls from his level and endeavors to regain his strength, he creates the souls of converts. This is like someone who wants to take his friend out of souls that they made in Haran," which is the three aspects of Elokim in Smallness,[24] having the numerical value of the word Haran.[25]

Degel Machane Ephraim, Vayera, p. 5

"I have put off my coat; how shall I put it on? I have washed my feet; how shall I defile them?"

Song of Songs 5:3

3.5 After the Tzaddik ascends Above, he descends again to uplift the lowest levels. This is the mystery of: "A righteous man falls seven times and rises." (*Proverbs 24:16*),[26] and of: "the souls that they had made in Haran."

This concept applies both to this world and the next, for the Tzaddik returns in subsequent

---

the mud. He also has to go down into the muck to raise him up."

[24] See R. Yitzchak Luria, *Etz Chayim, Sha'ar HaKelalim*, chapter 13.

[25] G•d's Name "Elokim" has the numerical value of 86. When multiplied by three, gives the number 258, which is the numerical value of the word "Haran." The implication is that when Abraham and Sarah were in the land of Haran — in a state of small mindedness — they gave birth to the souls of converts: "the souls that they had made in Haran."

[26] See *Tikunei Zohar*, at the end of *Tikun 32*.

LECH LECHA

incarnations to uplift those individuals who are offshoots[27] of his branches, so that they are all repaired.

However, at first, he does not want to come down, for he is afraid that he will not return and will come to sin. Thus, they promise him that he will not sin.

Toldot Yaakov Yosef, Chaya Sarah, p. 21b

"Whatever your hand can do by your strength, do . . ." *Ecclesiastes 9:10*

3.6 That is, in order to uplift people on [the level of] *Assiyah*[28] to [the level of] thought, which is known by the letter *yud*,[29] that also spells out the word *yado* — "his hand" (יד — ידו). This is by means of *Da'as*, which is the aspect of *Yosef*, as is known.

Ben Poras Yosef, p. 68d

---

[27] Literally, *nitzutzos* — sparks.
[28] The lowest of the spiritual worlds.
[29] As the first letter of the Tetragrammaton, the letter *yud* represents the world of thought, i.e. the beginning of creation. The letter *hey*, as the last letter of the Tetragrammaton, corresponds to *Malchus* and the world of *Asiyah*.

29

CHAPTER FOUR

VAYEIRA

"And he said, please my L•rd, if I have found favor in your eyes, do not pass by your servant."
Vayeira 18:3,4

4.1 Greater is welcoming in guests than receiving the face of the Shechinah. (*Shabbat 127a*)[30]

Even though welcoming guests sometimes wastes a person's time from Torah study, or can lead one to hear defamatory stories, it is still greater than receiving the Shechinah.

Toldot Yaakov Yosef, p. 109b

4.2 "Guest" — Oreyach (אורח) is Or Chet — the "Light of Eight" (אור ח'). Thus, Abraham received guests, for chet is the World to Come,[31] like a guest that comes. This is the World of Binah. Abraham was the Attribute of Kindness (Chesed), "the day of

---

[30] The Talmud deduces this from the use of the word L•rd in the above verse, which refers to G•d, and not one of the travelers. Abraham had been in a state of communion with G•d, but when the three travelers passed by, he asked G•d to wait while he tended to their needs.

[31] The number seven represent the completion of creation, as in the seven days of the week. The number eight (*chet*) represents one level above the creation, which is the transcendent World to Come. It also corresponds to the Sefirah of Binah, which is the eighth Sefirah when counting up from Malchus.

all days,"³² and the light of Chesed that passes through all the Sefiros.³³

Therefore, Abraham would bring the light of the *Chet* of *Binah,* into all the Sefiros.³⁴ And thus, he merited the entire Torah by means of the letter *hey* added to his name.³⁵ For this is the World of *Binah,* from where the Torah issues forth.

Degel Machane Ephraim, "Things I heard from my Grandfather"

4.3 I received from my grandfather [an explanation] of "commencing with [the honor of] the hosts of

---

32 See *Be'er Mayim Chayim,* on *parashas Yisro 19:6.*
33 See the writings of the Arizal in the laws on Succah.
34 The Sefirah of Chesed is one below the Sefirah of Binah and is the first the configuration of the lower seven Sefiros, from Chesed to Malchus. Thus, it draws from the light of Binah, which corresponds to the World to Come, and shines it into the Sefiros below.
35 The Sages say that Abraham knew and observed the entire Torah, as the verse says: "Because Abraham hearkened to My voice, and kept My charge, My commandments, My statutes, and My laws" (Genesis 26:5). According to the Baal Shem Tov, this is because G•d added the letter *hey* to his name, changing it from Abram to Abraham (אברם — אברהם). The first letter *hey* in the Tetragrammaton corresponds to the Sefirah of *Binah,* which is the source of the Torah.

Torah."³⁶ For the guest brings Torah to the host, and according to the guest is the nature of Torah that is revealed to him.

ibid, Vayeira

---

³⁶ *Berachos 83b*. The Talmud relates that when the Sages reassembled in the town of Yavneh after the destruction of Jerusalem, they opened their discourses with statements of thanks and respect for the local residents who made their homes available to the members of the gathering.

CHAPTER FIVE

CHAYA SARAH

GENESIS

"And Abraham was old, well advanced in years; and G•d had blessed Abraham with everything."

Chaya Sarah 24:1

5.1 Based upon what I heard from my grandfather on the verse: "It came to pass, when Solomon was old, that his wives turned away his heart after other gods . . . . ." (*I Kings 11:4*), we see from here that [when Abraham was old] "G•d had blessed Abraham with everything."

"Everything" — *bakol* — has the numerical value of *ben* — "son."[37]

The wise will understand this.[38]

Degel Machane Ephraim, Chayah Sarah

---

[37] The words בכל and בן both have the numerical value of 52.

[38] The verse says "For the ways of the L•rd are right; the just walk in them, but transgressors stumble in them." (*Hosea 14:10*) The Torah is comprised of two aspects — spirit and matter, revelation and concealment, the Tree of Life and the Tree of Knowledge. Thus, the Talmud states: "If a person is unworthy, the Torah becomes a potion of death for him; if he is worthy, it is a potion of life." (*Yoma 72b*) These two aspects also correspond to the spiritual paradigms of Giver and Receiver, or Lights and Vessels, and Kabbalistically, are represented by the Masculine and Feminine dimensions of creation. Only when they are united can harmony reign in the

CHAYA SARAH

5.2 There is no word in the Torah that cannot yield two interpretations,[39] which are the aspect of masculine and feminine. And thus, there is nothing created in the world that does not include everything, with free choice given to choose either aspect. Thus, "his wives turned away his heart."

Ben Poras Yosef, p. 14c

---

universe. Even then, however, the influence must be from above to below — from giver to receiver, spirit to matter. When the aspect of receiver dominates, then the vessel can be too strong, and the light can be concealed. This model applies to every word of the Torah, and is the meaning of the verse: ". . . his wives turned away his heart." Abraham, however, merited "everything," i.e. a son. He learned Torah from the side of light and revelation.

Along these lines, the *Degel Machane Ephraim* (*parashas Masai*) writes: "I heard from my grandfather, in the name of the *sefer Bris Menucha*, that if you see a Torah scholar who has incorrect opinions and acts improperly, he certainly has drunk from the 'bitter waters.'" Thus, the Rabbis taught in *Pirkei Avos 1:11*: "Sages, be careful with your words, lest you incur the penalty of exile, and be banished to a place of evil waters, and the disciples who follow you there will drink and die (spiritually) and consequently, the Name of Heaven will be desecrated."

[39] In *Ben Poras Yosef, p. 23d*, R. Yaakov Yosef writes: "In every word, there are two meanings, one of compassion, which is the aspect of the Masculine, and one of judgment, which is called the Feminine."

GENESIS

"And [Lavan] said [to Eliezer]: 'Come in, you blessed of G•d.'" *Chaya Sarah 24:31*

The Midrash states: "Because he served that Tzaddik (Abraham) faithfully, he left the category of the cursed, and entered the category of the blessed."[40]

5.3 The Baal Shem Tov said that even a non Jew who eats something which contains a holy spark, and then serves a Jew with the vitality he gets from that food, elevates the spark to some degree, though not as much as if a Jew would eat it.

Me'or Einayim, Matos

"Now, I came this day to the well . . . ." *Chaya Sarah 24:42*

"Today I left (Haran) and today I arrived." From here

---

[40] *Bereshit Rabbah 60:7*. According to the Midrash, Abraham's servant, Eliezer, was a descendent of Canaan, of who it was said: "Cursed is Canaan, a servant of servants he will be to his brothers." (Genesis 9:25)

[we learn that] the way was shortened for him.[41] Rabbi Eliezer said, "The common talk of the servants of the Forefathers is better than the Torah of their descendents."[42] *Rashi*

5.4 This very verse is the source of the Divine Name that causes *kefitzas haderech*. This is the meaning of: "Today I left (Haran) and today I arrived." From here, the way was shortened for him." From here precisely! From these very words that he said!

This is the meaning of "The common talk of the servants of the Forefathers is better than the Torah of their descendents." For their words hint to wondrous mysteries and Unifications to shorten the way, which is not true of their descendents, even by means of the Torah they study.

Avodas Yisroel, Genesis

---

[41] *Kefitzat Haderech* — a miraculous shortening of a journey, in which great distances are covered in a short amount of time.

[42] Eliezer relates the events surrounding his meeting with Rivkah several times in great detail. This is the common talk of the servants of the Forefathers. In other chapters, however, the Torah is so sparse with words that dozens of laws must be derived from the nuances of a single verse, as the Talmud states concerning the laws of Shabbos that they are like mountains hanging by hairs; i.e. huge amounts of laws are derived from very few words.

CHAPTER SIX

TOLDOT

GENESIS

"These are the generations of Isaac, the son of Abraham. Abraham gave birth to Isaac." *Toldot 25:19*

6.1 This verse contains a question and its answer. The question is, how did Isaac, who represents the forces of limitation, come from Abraham, who is the aspect of loving kindness?[43] The answer is "Abraham gave birth to Isaac." That is, the forces of limitation derive from those of loving kindness, in order that there should be concealment in the world. Because when one person lacks something, and another person gives it to him, the world becomes founded on loving kindness. "You have built a world of love." (*Psalms 89:3*) This draws down forces of loving kindness into the world.

Mevaser Tzedek, Behar

---

[43] According to Kabbalah, the seven lower sefirot, from Chesed to Malchut, correspond to seven central Biblical figures. Abraham corresponds to Chesed, which represents the forces of love and expansion. Isaac corresponds to Gevurah, which embodies the forces of contraction and concealment.

TOLDOT

"And Jacob was a simple man, a dweller in tents. (Now, I came this day to the well . . .)"
Toldot 25:27

"The steps of a man are arranged by G•d, who delights in his way. Though he falls, he shall not be cast down." *Psalms 37:23, 24*

6.2 A person must do everything possible to perfect himself. He must examine his personality traits and his opinions to see if he is flawed in any way. Thus, the verse says: "Seek peace and pursue it." (*Psalms 34:15*) That is, look into yourself to see if you have flaws, and seek to perfect yourself in that area.[44] However, this only applies to a person who can perfect himself, if he cannot, he should "pursue it" — perhaps he will find a wise man who can help him fix himself.

At times, a person can perfect himself where he lives, in his town, without needing to travel afar, for parts of himself have not fallen there.[45] At other

---

[44] The root of the Hebrew word for peace, *SHaLoM*, is the same as that for the word perfection, *SHeLeiMot*.
[45] According to the writings of the Arizal, when G•d created the world, due to a flaw in creation, sparks of holiness were dispersed throughout the world. It was the job of Adam to reunite these sparks with their

times, though parts of his life force have fallen to other places where he must travel to redeem them, he can extract them all with the greatness of his Torah, because Torah study is equal to everything. Thus it says: "The Torah of G•d is perfect, it restores the soul" (Psalms 19:8), that is, by means of the Torah a person learns, he can restore the lost fragments of his soul. It also says: "One who studies Torah selflessly, merits many things."[46] That is, he merits to extract the life force from all places, because all these places themselves were created from the Torah.[47]

---

source. When Adam sinned, he cause even more sparks to be scattered, and the job of collecting them fell to all of humanity, and ultimately, to the Jewish people. This explains the reason for the many exiles the Jewish people have suffered — their purpose was to regain the lost sparks of holiness. The Baal Shem Tov implies here that this process occurs on the individual level as well as the cosmic level; that is, each soul, on descending into this world, also experiences a dispersal of essential sparks, which must be regained in the course of one's life, and integrated into the service of G•d.

[46] *Pirkei Avot 6:*

[47] The Midrash states that G•d looked in the Torah and created the world, and that He used to Torah as a blueprint of reality (*Bereishit Rabbah 1*). Since all reality is based upon the Torah, a person who learns Torah can extract the sparks of soul that are scattered in all places of the world.

However, it is rare to find a person who can do this. This was the quality of Jacob, who could extract the life force scattered in all places by means of his Torah study. Thus, he was "a simple man, who dwelt in tents."[48] Though he studied Torah in his one tent, where he lived, it was as if he dwelt in many places and many tents.

Others, however, must travel to different places in order to repair their life force. Sometimes a person wishes to travel to one destination, yet ends up arriving somewhere else. This is no accident, for he must repair his life force that has fallen there. At times, it may be enough to merely eat or drink in that place, in order to perfect himself.

Ohr HaChochmah, Vayera

"And Isaac loved Esau, because (he provided) his mouth with game." *Toldot 25:28*

6.4 Rashi explains that Esau trapped and deceived Isaac with his words. The Baal Shem Tov

---

[48] The verse uses the plural. Rashi explains that this means the study halls of the prophets Shem and Ever.

commented on this,⁴⁹ that from the day Esau deceived Isaac, no Tzaddik has ever been able to see bad in his children.

Zohar Chai, Vayeshev p. 346a

"Because Abraham obeyed My voice, and kept My charge: My commandments, My statutes, and My laws." *Toldot 26:5*

6.5 Rashi explains that Abraham observed the commandments of both the Written Torah and the Oral Torah. How is this possible?

Our Sages have said that in the future, the commandments will be annuled.⁵⁰ I heard from my grandfather [the Baal Shem Tov], in his name or in the name of the Ramban, that in the future, human beings will experience the spiritual vitality that lies within each mitzvah, and how it is the very life force of the soul and of all the worlds. This is the meaning of the verse: "If My covenant is not upheld day and night, then the laws of heaven and earth I have not established." (*Jeremiah 33:25*) "My

---

⁴⁹ Recorded by the Chasidic master, Rabbi Michael of Zlotichov.
⁵⁰ *Nidah 61b*.

TOLDOT

covenant" refers to the Torah.[51] Abraham apprehended the entire Torah by himself, not as a commandment — because the Torah had not yet been given — rather, he understood how the life force of each mitzvah is the very vitality of the soul, and he knew that he needed to fulfill them in order to cling to the life of all lives.

On the future world, the verse says: "The earth will be filled with the knowledge of G•d, as the sea is covered with water." (Isaiah 11:9). This is also the meaning of the verse, "Your eyes will behold your teacher." (Isaiah 30:20) For then, everything will be revealed — the source of the commandments and all their inner secrets, how they illuminate and enliven human beings and all the worlds, and how it is impossible to reach human perfection without them.

Then, everyone will apprehend the path of life, as did our father, Abraham.

Degel Machane Ephraim, Tzav

---

[51] The Baal Shem Tov understands this verse as saying that the vitality of the creation is derived from the Torah, and that only by upholding the latter, can the former continue to exist.

GENESIS

"Now all the wells that his father's servants had dug while Abraham was still alive, the Philistines had sealed them up, and filled them with earth." *Toldot 26:15*

6.6 This is the mystery of all the wells that the Forefathers dug in order to find water — meaning Torah — in the "earth" — i.e. on the lowest level.[52] For each of them, by perfecting his character traits, brought forth a revelation of Torah — "a well of living water" *Toldot 26:19* — from the earth and the lowest levels, so that it not be covered over again.

However, after Abraham died, these revelations were sealed up by the "earth" that covered the "water." This was due to the Philistines — the impure shells that reasserted themselves. But Isaac came and redug the wells, as it is written: "He redug the wells that had been dug in the days of his father Abraham." *Toldot 26:18* This too refers to the revelation of Torah by Abraham and Isaac. And even today, Torah lies hidden in those very deeds of Abraham and Isaac.

---

[52] Water is a common metaphor for Torah, as in the verse: "Ho, every one that thirsts, come you for water..." (*Isaiah 55:1*). Earth is considered the lowest of the four elements of fire, air, water and earth.

TOLDOT

And all of this was to repair the future generations. For were it not for the Forefathers, it would be impossible to have any understanding of Torah, and to draw close to G•d at all.

Me'or Einayim, Vayetze

"He then moved away from there and dug another well, and this time it was not disputed, so he named it Rechovos ("Expansiveness"), and he said: 'Now G•d has broadened us, and we shall be fruitful in the land.'" *Toldot 26:22*

6.7 Inner fear [of G•d] is called "Rechovos," for there is no fear of the *kelipot* there, so that one must limit oneself because of them — through suffering, small mindedness and [self] afflictions to prevent them from leeching on to holiness. Rather, "Now G•d has broadened us" with the inner essence of fear that is called Rechovos. Then "we shall be fruitful in the land" — we will give forth fruits, to turn the multitude from sin, to be a Rabbi and a Rebbe, to uplift and create souls. However, if a person is a Rabbi or Rebbe yet lacks inner fear, he is from the *kelipot nogah*.

Leket Imrei Peninim, p. 209b

GENESIS

"And Jacob went out from Be'er Sheva, and went toward Haran." *Toldot 27:10*

6.8 The Midrash quotes Jacob as saying: "'I will lift my eyes to the mountains. From where will my help come?' (*Psalms 121:1*). What! Have I lost hope in my Creator? G•d forbid, I certainly have not lost hope in Him; rather 'My help comes from G•d, who made heaven and earth.'" (*Psalms 121:2*)[53]

This teaches us that when the Heavenly Court wants to mete out punishment to a person, they first take away his trust in G•d.[54] It is therefore wise to beseech G•d to strengthen out trust in Him.

Toldot Yaakov Yosef, Misphotim

---

[53] Bereishit Rabbah 68:2.
[54] This teaching reflects a central Chassidic idea that faith in G•d as the one, true Ruler of creation can actually draw down His beneficent guidance into our lives. As long as a person completely believes in G•d's Providence, no other force in the world can harm him. Thus, when heaven seeks to punish someone, they first take away this trust. How good if we could have it always! The *Degel Machane Ephraim, parashas Ekev*, adds to this teaching (in the name of the Baal Shem Tov), that G•d never sends afflictions to a person, unless He first throws them into depression.

TOLDOT

"And he dreamt, and behold a ladder set upon the earth, with its top reaching heaven, and behold, the angels of G•d ascended and descended on it."

Toldot 27:12

6.9 The Hebrew word for "ladder," *sulam*, has the same numerical value as the word for "money" *mamon*.[55] This ladder — money — is set upon the earth, as it is a very material thing, yet its "top" reaches heaven, for it can bring a person eternal reward. "The angels of G•d ascended and descended on it." This refers to human beings.[56] Some ascend to great heights through the proper use of money, and some descend to the depths of hell, as the verse says, "Wealth safeguards its owner for his detriment." (*Proverbs 5:12*)

Turei Zahav, VaYetze

---

[55] 136.
[56] Human beings can also be called "Angels," which means "messenger" in Hebrew, because their role, too, is to carry out the will of G•d in this world. See *Ben Poras Yosef, parashas VaYetze,* by Rabbi Yaakov Yosef of Polnoye.

GENESIS

"[Rabbi Akiva] used to say: Everything is given on collateral,[57] and a net is spread over all the living . . . . ." *Pirkei Avos 3:16*

6.10 The Hebrew word "spread" (*prusa*), is from the word *pras* "reward,"[58] which itself is related to the word "livelihood," *parnasa*. The net of *parnasa* is spread over the entire world. Everyone is so preoccupied with making a living that no one has the time to think about serving G•d.

Bas Ayin, Bamidbar

"I am the L•rd, G•d of Abraham, your father, and G•d of Isaac." *Toldot 27:13*

6.11 This is why we say in our prayers: "G•d of Abraham, G•d of Isaac [and G•d of Jacob]," and not "G•d of Abraham, Isaac [and Jacob]." For a person should never rely on the spiritual searching and path of worship of his fathers, just as Isaac and Jacob did not rely upon the conclusions that their

---

[57] That is, a person is responsible for everything he has in life, and in the end, must give an accounting on all that he did.

[58] As in: "Do not be like servants who serve their master in order to receive reward — *pras*" (*Pirkei Avos 1:3*).

TOLDOT

father Abraham reached. Each one sought to understand the oneness of G•d for himself, and to reach his own conclusions as to how to serve Him. Thus, we link G•d's name with each of the forefathers individually.

Korban Ha'Ani, Bechukosai

6.12 It is known that the Forefathers corresponded to the sefirot of Chesed, Gevurah and Tiferet. Abraham embodied the quality of Chesed — loving kindness. He loved and showed generosity to the entire creation, and tried to instill in them faith in G•d, and a desire to serve Him; because the trait of Chesed corresponds to love. Through Abraham's great dedication to this trait, he came to recognize and comprehend the Creator, and realize that G•d runs the entire world.

Isaac learned and received this approach from Abraham; however, he still wanted to come to his own understanding of G•d. This is as the verse says: "*Know the G•d of your fathers, and serve Him.*" (*I Chronicles 28:9*) One should not merely accept this service as a tradition, to be fulfilled by rote.[59] Therefore, Isaac devoted himself to the trait

---

[59] That is, each person must come to his own knowledge of G•d. In Chassidus, the word *da'at*, "knowledge," also

GENESIS

of piety.[60] And out of his great care [to fulfill the will of G•d], he came to know and comprehend G•d for himself, besides what he received from his father.

Now, Jacob realized that there must be a middle way in the operation of the world, that mediated between Chesed and Gevurah, because the world could not survive if it can only function according to one of these two extremes. Therefore, he devoted himself to the trait of Tiferet.[61] Through this, he arrived at a deeper perception of G•d than his fathers, and is called the "Chosen of the Forefathers."[62] He saw that the world could not exist in unmitigated judgment, and so tempered it with the trait of Compassion.[63]

---

has the connotation of mystical union. The use of the word *da'at* for union can be first found in *Genesis 4:1*: "And Adam *knew* Eve, his wife." And concerning the days of the Messiah, the verse says: "The earth will be filled with the knowledge of G•d, as the sea is covered with water." (*Isaiah 11:9*) referring to a direct, mystical knowledge of G•d that all humanity will then experience.

[60] Literally "fear," that corresponds to the sefirah of Gevurah.

[61] Tiferet means "beauty" or "splendor," and is positioned below and between the sefirot of Chesed and Gevurah. It includes them both, and mediates between them.

[62] *Pesikta Rabotai, Vayishlach 76*.

[63] Judgment, *Din*, is associated with the sefirah of Gevurah, because it has the implication of restriction

TOLDOT

Likutey Yakarim, p. 9b

"May G•d grant you the dew of heaven and the fat of the earth, much grain and wine." *Toldot 27:28*

6/13 Rabbi Levi said: All the good that enters the world comes only in the merit of the Jewish nation. All the rain that falls is in their merit. All the dew that drops is in their merit. As it says: May G•d grand you the dew of heaven and the fat of the earth." "Grant *you*" — in your merit, and upon you it depends.[64]

---

and uncompromising demands. Compassion is considered an admixture of Chesed — love, and Gevurah — judgment. Because, whereas pure Chesed gives uncompromisingly, and pure Gevurah withholds absolutely, Compassion gives in accordance with the needs of the receiver, neither totally overwhelming, nor denying. The Baal Shem Tov is also alluding to the Midrash that states that G•d first sought to create the world with the attribute of Judgment. When He saw that it could not stand, he added the attribute of Compassion. Likewise, Jacob saw that the world could not serve G•d following the extreme patterns of Abraham and Isaac, and so combined them in the trait of compassion, which enables all creatures to find a place in the worship of G•d.

[64] *Bereishit Rabbah 66:2.*

GENESIS

6.14 The Talmud's states: "Every day, a heavenly voice proclaims: 'The entire world is sustained on account of (beshevil) my son, Chanina,[65] and my son Chanina makes do with a kav of carobs from week to week."[66] That is, the Tzaddik is like a path and a pipeline that carries fluids. Through his holy deeds, he draws down bounty to the entire world. And just as the pipe takes no pleasure from what passes through it, likewise, the Tzaddik's only will and desire is to bestow upon others. And this is what the heavenly voice declares: "The entire world is sustained b'shevil — that is, in the channel that my son, Chanina, makes."[67] For he is like a path and a channel that thinks nothing of its own good, but suffices with a little: ". .with a kav of carobs from week to week."[68] *Avodas Yisroel, Likutim*[69]

---

[65] Rabbi Chanina ben Dosa.
[66] *Berachos* 17b.
[67] The word *shevil* means "path." Thus, the word *beshevil* ("on account of") can be read as "in the path of" (ב"שביל). The *Toldot Yaakov Yosef* writes: "Moses, our Teacher, opened the path of fear [of G•d] in the world, and Aharon opened the path of love. Likewise, Chanina ben Dosa opened the path of livelihood in the world, as I heard from my Teacher: 'The whole world is nourished through the path of Chanina ben Dosa.'"
[68] See *Toldot Yaakov Yosef,* p. 173b: "[Chanina] did not want to benefit from this world, and so others take

TOLDOT

---

benefit from his sustenance, while he will take benefit in the World to Come."

[69] The quote from *Bereishit Rabbah* 66:2 is taken from a parallel teaching in the sefer *Tzafnah Paneach*, by Rabbi Yaakov Yosef of Polnoye.

CHAPTER SEVEN

VAYEITZEI

GENESIS

"The land upon which you lie, I will give to you . . ." *Vayeitzei 28:13*

7.1 Rashi states that G•d folded up the entire land of Israel under Jacob's head.[70] This means that Jacob would not have to travel from place to place to retrieve his sparks, but could find them in his place.[71]

Ben Poras Yosef, p. 18b

7.2 Jacob was the aspect of Truth, which is the beginning, middle and end.[72] This is the meaning of

---

[70] Based upon the Talmud, Chulin 9ab.

[71] See the Baal Shem Tov on parashat Toldot: *Genesis 25:27*. Rabbi Yaakov Yosef of Polnoye explains: "This is accomplished through *da'at*, that is, when a person concentrates on the letters of his Torah study and prayers, and knows how to cull out the sparks that fell in the 'breaking of the vessels,' by means of these letters".

[72] The sefirah of Tiferet also corresponds to the trait of Truth. Thus the verse says, "Give truth to Jacob (Tiferet), kindness to Abraham (Chesed)." (*Micah 7:20*) Truth is called the "beginning, middle and end," because the Hebrew letters that comprise the word Truth — Emet, are *aleph*, *mem*, and *tav*, the first, middle and last letters of the alphabet. The Baal Shem Tov seems to means that since Jacob corresponds to truth, which embraces the entire alphabet, he can redeem the fallen sparks without effort. This is similar to what the Baal

VAYEITZEI

G•d's folding up the Land of Israel under him, so that he didn't have to exert himself at all to separate out the sparks.

Degel Machane Ephraim, Bechukosai

"Surely, G•d is in this place, and I did not know it!" *Vayeitzei 28:16*

7.3 Meaning, "If I had known it, I would not have slept here."[73] That is, if a person knows how to unite this trait, it would not be called sleep.[74]

Katones Passim, p. 35a

Shem Tov said about the Torah (which also corresponds to Jacob and Truth), that through study alone, one can redeem the sparks in one's place, without having to travel afar. See the previous footnote.

[73] See Rashi's comment on this verse.

[74] This refers to a very deep and central teaching of the Baal Shem Tov; that the attribute of *da'at* — knowledge of G•d — has the ability to cut through all levels of darkness and confusion immediately. *Da'at* is the ability to remember G•d, on whatever level a person is on. According to this teaching, a person only needs to remember that the spiritual darkness they are in is *also* from G•d, and that G•d is as present there as He is in the moments of inspiration, to be immediately catapulted to a level of closeness to G•d, and the dissipation of the darkness; for distance from G•d *only* comes into existence because we fail to remember that it

GENESIS

"Jacob awoke from his sleep, and said 'Surely, G•d is in this place, but I did not know it.' And he was afraid, and said. 'How awesome is this

---

too is from Him. Rabbi Yaakov Yosef writes: "If [Jacob] knew he was in the aspect of small — mindedness and sleep (a synonym for spiritual unconsciousness), he could unite this level *also* [with G•d], and it would no longer be called the aspect of sleep." A famous parable of the Baal Shem Tov illustrates this point:

There was once a king who wanted to test the loyalty of his servants in all the distant lands of his reign. He sent a fleet of his ships across the ocean, bearing the flags of an enemy nation. When the fleet drew close to each port, it sent a message to the citizens of the town, "You have five days to surrender, or we will destroy you."

In every town there was panic. In some towns, the people prepared for war. "We are loyal citizens of the king, and we will fight for him to the death." In other towns, they were ready to surrender, "The king is so far from here, he has nothing to do with our lives. Why should we die for him?"

However, in one town, the people calmly replied, "This is a test! We love our king. He need not test us!"
The challenge of the battles represents the evil inclination in man, that seeks to seduce him to transgress G•d's will. Some people fight it, while others give in. In both cases, a test exists, because the individual forgets that the side of evil is also from G•d, and merely testing him. As soon as a person realizes that the tests is itself from G•d, and not something outside of Him, the test itself disappears, and one comes close to G•d again.

VAYEITZEI

place! This alone is G•d's house, and this is the gate to heaven.'" *Vayeitzei 28:16, 17*

7.4 There is a problem [with this verse]. Had another person been standing there claiming that it was not G•d's house, but another house, such as an inn or something similar, it would have been correct to tell him: "It's not as you say. This alone is G•d's house!" But since there was no one there to contradict him, why did he say it that way? He should have said: "This is surely G•d's house!"

This can be explained with the Gemara: "Rabbi Yinai proclaimed, 'Woe to one who lacks a courtyard, but makes a gate to the courtyard!'"[75] According to Rashi, the Torah is the gate that leads to the fear of G•d.[76] Now, it is known that before going to Haran, Jacob learned Torah for fourteen years in the study hall of Shem [and Ever].[77] Yet, during that entire time, he never felt the awe of G•d that he felt on Mount Moriah, the place of the Holy Temple.[78] Therefore, he said, "Since I see how

---

[75] *Shabbat 31b*. Meaning, woe to one who studies Torah (the "gate"), but has no fear of G•d (the "courtyard").
[76] *Yoma 72b*.
[77] *Megilah 17a*.
[78] The Midrash states that Jacob slept at the place of the future Holy Temple. See Rashi on the verses above.

awesome this place is, I decree and declare that this alone is G•d's house. This is His main dwelling place. As it says: 'My house shall be a house of prayer . . . . .' (*Isaiah 56:7*)[79] And all that I learned in the study hall of Shem is only the gate to heaven; it is only the gate to fear.

Kesser Shem Tov, part 2, p. 5c

"And Jacob made a vow, saying 'If G•d will be with me, and will protect me on the journey that I am taking, if He gives me bread to eat and clothing to wear, so that I return to my father's house in peace, then Hashem shall be my G•d.'"
Vayeitzei 28:20,21

7.5 "In all your ways know Him" (*Proverbs 3:6*) — whether things are going well or not. For when misfortune befalls a person, G•d forbid, he should think that it comes to atone for his sins.

However, when a Tzaddik experiences good, he should worry that he is using up his merits. This is the meaning of: ". . . . . then Hashem (Y — H — V — H) shall be my G•d (Elokim)." Perhaps, [thought

---

[79] The Baal Shem Tov puts this verse in the mouth of Jacob, as if he said it.

Jacob], the name Y — H — V — H, which represents the attribute of compassion, is in fact Elokim — the attribute of Strict Judgment. Therefore, I must constantly add to my merit.

Tzava'as HaRivash, p. 12b; Ohr Torah, Vayetze

"And Jacob lifted up his feet." *Vayeitzei 29:1*

7.6 These are the aspect of the lowest levels. For when Tzaddikim experience a state of constricted consciousness, they uplift the sparks that are relegated to the lowest levels.

Degel Machane Ephraim, Vayetze

"Rachel was shapely and beautiful to look at. And Jacob loved Rachel . . . . ." *Vayeitzei 29:17,18*

7.7 This was because Jacob had the attribute of Tiferet ("Beauty").[80] Whenever he saw something attractive, he would say: "If this beauty so becomes

---

[80] According to Kabbalah, Abraham corresponded to the Sefirah of Chesed — Love; Isaac corresponded to the Sefirah of Gevurah — Strength; and Jacob corresponded to the Sefirah of Tiferet — Beauty or Harmony.

a physical thing, how much higher would it be if it was dedicated to praising and glorifying G•d.

Ohr Torah, Vayeitzei

"He took along his kinsmen and pursued [Jacob] for seven days, and he overtook him in the Gilead Mountains." *Vayeitzei 31:23*

7.8 It is known that mystically, Jacob corresponds to Da'at,[81] for the aspects of Jacob and Moses are identical.[82] The only difference is that one is within and the other without, one is the inner aspect of Da'at, and the other, the outer aspect of Da'at.

Now, before Jacob went to the House of Lavan, Da'at and Torah were in concealment. Numerous fundaments of Torah[83] were scattered on the lowest levels because Da'at was not revealed in the world. Many of them were concealed in the house of Laban. These were the very words of Torah that are written in the sefer Torah describing Jacob's deeds while there.

---

[81] Da'at means mystical cognition of G•d.
[82] Moses also corresponds to the Sefirah of Da'at. See *Zohar 2:221a*.
[83] I.e. essential, unformulated elements of Torah.

VAYEITZEI

These deeds held the potential Torah that Jacob removed and purified from the depth of the *kelipot* of Laban; for though his *kelipot* was great, Jacob extracted all of them during the twenty years he was there.

Thus, when Laban pursued Jacob, it was because some Torah still remained hidden within him. This made up the very verses that describe his pursuit and debate with Jacob, until the end of the parasha. The Torah in these verses remained clothed in Laban, for Jacob had not yet removed them. G•d therefore caused Laban to pursue Jacob, in order to bring him the Torah that had not yet been fully removed. When he overtook Jacob, and spoke the words that are written, Jacob extracted them all, until nothing remained. For everything that happened with Laban, and all the events recorded in the verses, was all Torah and *avodas Hashem*. [His going there] was all in order to reveal Torah from the aspect of Haran, which is the depths of the impure shells, to cause a revelation of holiness, and include it in the supernal Torah.

Me'or Einayim, Vayeitzei

CHAPTER EIGHT

VAYISHLACH

GENESIS

"And the messengers returned to Jacob and said, 'We came to your brother Esau, and he is also coming to meet you, and four hundred men are with him.' Then Jacob was very afraid and distressed" *Vayishlach 32:7,8*

8.1 The verse says: "May only goodness and kindness pursue me all the days of my life." (*Psalms 23:6*) A person does not always know what is good for him; for who is wise enough to think that they always know what is in their best interest? Sometimes, the goodness even runs after a person. G•d, in His mercy, wants to shine His light, deliverance and success upon him; yet the person has no idea that he would benefit from this thing and be successful, and so he turns around and runs away from what is for his own good.

Therefore, with holy inspiration, King David asked on behalf of all Israel, "May only goodness and kindness pursue me." Even when I don't have enough insight to accept these things in my life, and, in fact, I run away from them; still, I beg You that they should run after me, until they overtake

VAYISHLACH

me, and I welcome them and bring blessing into my life.[84]   Likutey Torah, Ki Tavo

---

[84] This teaching reflects the idea that even apparently negative occurrences are actually for our own good. G•d's nature is ultimately loving and beneficent, and therefore, even suffering will ultimately be revealed to have been for our benefit. Indeed, Kabbalah teaches that there are many things that can *only* be repaired through suffering, such as purification from certain sins. In such as case, Divine blessing would only come *after* the experience of purification. However, the Baal Shem Tov, in his great love for the Jewish people, propounded yet another principle: G•d is all powerful, and can therefore accomplish the same repair that suffering achieves through loving means. The Baal Shem Tov composed the following prayer that reflects this idea: "I know that even the bad is for my good. However, You are G•d, and not a man, and you can transform the bad to real good, so that even though there won't be any aspect of bad left, even so, it will be completely for my benefit, so that the necessary repair can come from the good itself." (See *Mishmeret Yitamar, Vayishlach.*)

This can be understood with a parable taught be the Baal Shem Tov:

Once, a simple country villager rebelled against the king. Everyone was sure that he would be caught and sentenced to death. However, the king did something else. As soon as he learnt of the rebellion, he appointed the villager to be mayor of his town. Later, he appointed him to a higher position, and then to an even higher one, until he made him one of the dukes of the land. However, the more he promoted the man, the worse the man felt for having originally rebelled against the king, who showed him so much kindness. This was

GENESIS

"And he touched the hollow of his (Jacob's) thigh, and his thigh was put out of joint, as he wrestled with him." *Vayishlach 32:26*

8.2 "There are those who toil at Torah, with no one to support them, or put money in their pocket; therefore, the Torah is forgotten in every generation, and the strength of Torah is weakened every day."
Zohar, parashas Vayishlach, p. 171a

8.3 I heard a parable from my grandfather [the Baal Shem Tov]. When a king wages war, he uses many types of soldiers, such as foot soldiers, and horsemen. According to the rules of war, it is the foot soldiers who enter the heat of the battle. They may even be chained together, so that they cannot disperse and flee, but must stand and fight. The horsemen are also involved in the battle; however, when the fighting becomes too dangerous, they

---

the king's intention. For had he punished the man once at first, the man's pain would not have been as great as that which he felt over a long period of time, in the face of the king's continual beneficence. Likewise, when a person sins, G•d showers upon him even more grace than before. When the person realizes G•d's goodness to him, despite his behavior, he is immediately humbled and repents of all that he is doing wrong. (See *Otzar Mishle Chasidim, vol. 1, p. 85*).

VAYISHLACH

escape, and do not risk their lives. The foot soldiers, however, risk their lives for the honor of the king.

Yet, when they win the war, with G•d's help, it is the horsemen who return and carry off all of the spoils, as much as their horses can bear. Whereas the foot soldiers do not take more than a little bread and water to keep themselves alive for another day. They cannot carry heavy booty, and are satisfied just to sustain their lives. They trust that in the time of peace, the horsemen will give them whatever they need, for they certainly deserve the larger portion of the spoils. Furthermore, all of them are serving the same king, and it was they who risked their lives to win the war, for the sake of his honor. However, when that time comes, the horsemen do not agree, and do not want to share their bounty — not even a single meal, for they claim that the victory was on account of them.

What does this parable mean? The foot soldiers are spiritual people,[85] who constantly serve

---

[85] Literally, "men of form," *anshei tzurah*, as opposed to "men of substance," *anshei chomer*. The Baal Shem Tov uses the classic distinction between "form" and "substance," the spiritual and the material, to describe the two types of people. Rabbi Yaakov Yosef of Polnoye writes that there is an inherent conflict between the physical and the spiritual. Whereas the spiritual is

G•d, and give their lives for the honor of the king — the King of the world. *They* win the war, and defeat all the accusing forces that rise against them and try to prevent blessing from reaching this world. It is because of them that material bounty descends into this world. The horsemen are physical people, who ride on large and good horses; that is, their

---

drawn to high ideals and seeks to unite with its G•dly source, the physical is drawn after material desires and lower cravings. The test in life is not to abandon the physical, but to uplift it so that it too can serve G•d. This is done when the physical is used in the service of the soul, such as in the performance of the commandments, giving charity, and other good deeds. And just as this applies to each individual, so does it apply to human beings as a whole: there are those who are involved in spiritual pursuits, and those who follow after material gain. When the latter lend financial support to the former, then together, they form one body whose direction in life is transcendence and G•dliness. Not only that, but since all material wealth descends from the spiritual realm, both will be blessed materially as well. However, when "men of substance" do not support the "men of form," then both of them can fall away from the spiritual realm. According to the Zohar, this is the meaning of the struggle between Jacob and the angel (who was the guardian angel of Esau). Although Jacob, the man of the spirit, subdued him, he still caused Jacob harm by inflicting his legs, which represent the financial supporters of Torah — those who put Torah scholars "on their feet."

good fate.[86] When the war is won, and bounty flows into this world, they grab most of it; whereas the spiritual people make due with just enough for one day, as is the way of the Torah, and all those who trust in G•d. They are satisfied that they won the war, and that the king's honor will be exalted, and they assume that the physical people will provide for their needs, since the spiritual people are really the more important of the two. However, material people don't see it that way, and don't want to give them anything. "All the bounty belongs to us," they say. Eventually, though, the King will take notice, and will look upon His servants and their actions. Then, in His great goodness, He will certainly reward them with all manner of goodness and prosperity; for He knows the truth, that the victory depended upon them, and that they deserve all the rewards and bounty that descended in the first place.

Degel Machane Ephraim p. 96

"The messengers returned to Jacob with the report: 'We came to your brother Esau, and he is also heading toward you. He has 400 men with

---

[86] Literally, their good constellations.

him.' And Jacob was very frightened and distressed . . . . ." *Vayishlach 32:7,8*

8.4 It is written: "And like the fear of You, so is Your wrath." (*Psalms 90:11*) Meaning, a person should fear G•d at all times, just as when he is in distress,[87] for then he fears G•d greatly.

The verse can also be interpreted in reverse. In a time of distress, do not merely be afraid [due to the situation], for it is proper to feel the fear of G•d always.[88]

Likutim Yikarim, p. 4c

"And when he saw that he could not defeat him, he touched the hollow of [Jacob's] thigh; and Jacob's hip joint became dislocated as he wrestled with him." *Vayishlach 32:26*

8.5 I heard from my Master [the Baal Shem Tov], an explanation of the Mishnah: "When the spirits of a person's fellowmen are pleased (*nocha*) with him,

---

[87] I.e. in a time of G•d's wrath.
[88] Even when a person is afraid of a mortal danger, he should realize that the situation is being orchestrated by G•d; thus, it is G•d whom he should fear, not the situation itself.

G•d is pleased with him, and when the spirits of a person's fellowmen are not pleased with him, G•d is not pleased with him."[89] A human being is a microcosm, as is the entire Jewish nation.[90] One individual corresponds to the head, another, to the foot. Thus, we find the "heads of the generation,"[91] or the "eyes of the congregation."[92] When the head of the generation makes himself into a vessel for the presence of the Shechinah, it radiates from him to the rest of his generation. Thus, the Mishnah can be read: "When the spirits of a person's fellowmen rest upon them (*nocha*) from him,"[93] it is because the spirit of G•d rests upon the entire world through him.

The opposite is also true. If the spirit of G•d does not rest upon them, he is to blame, and not the generation.

---

[89] *Pirkei Avos* 3:10.
[90] That is, the entire Jewish people correspond to the human structure. (The words "as is the entire Jewish nation" are an addition from the parallel teaching in *Kesser Shem Tov*, p. 11d.)
[91] As in *Numbers 13:3*.
[92] As in *Numbers 15:24 and 20:27*.
[93] I.e., when the people are uplifted by an indwelling of spirit.

Although this isn't the Baal Shem Tov's exact words, it captures their meaning.
>Toldot Yaakov Yosef, p. 98a

8.6 The whole world comprises one complete form, a complete persona, in the mystery of world, year and soul.[94] Whatever is in the particular is also in the general. For instance, just as a single person is made up of substance and form,[95] so too, a city or a country. The heads of the people are the "form" and the soul of their generation, while the rest of the people are the "substance." Therefore, the Talmud comments on the verse, "This is the generation of those that seek Him," (*Psalms 24:6*) that "the generation follows those who seek Him, and those who seek Him follow the generation."[96] Because the purity of the body is according to the purity of the

---

[94] According to the *Sefer Yetzirah 6:1*, these are the three basic components of all reality: space, time and the human soul, and whatever exists on one dimension is reflected equally in the others. Thus, whatever exists in the world exists in history and in the soul.
[95] This follows the classic division of reality into matter and form, with the latter giving shape to the former.
[96] *Archin 17a.*

soul. If the soul is dirty, the body will be even more so, and visa versa.[97]

Moses embodied the mystery of Da'at.[98] Therefore, his generation was called the "Generation of Knowledge" (*dor de'ah*). Every generation is like this. Thus, a person who wants to repair the general must first repair the particular. By fixing himself, and transforming his own substance into form, others will naturally awaken in repentance, for they are included in him. Then, he will easily fix his generation, and transform substance into form. Thus, the Talmud says: "I would be surprised if there is anyone in this generation who can accept rebuke."[99] That is, if a preacher rebukes his audience, and does not include himself in his words, he will not make an impression on them at all.

Toldot Yaakov Yosef, p. 100a

8.7 All of Israel is one entity: some individuals are matter and some form. And just as matter, which is the body, needs the soul, so the soul needs the

---

[97] If the body would be pure, the soul would be even purer.
[98] "Knowledge" — meaning the direct, mystical knowledge of G•d.
[99] *Archin 17a*.

body. Therefore, do not separate yourself from [the people]. Unite with them and lead them with compassion, and return them to the good

Toldot Yaakov Yosef, p. 100c

CHAPTER NINE

VAYESHEV

GENESIS

". . . . . and Joseph brought [the brothers'] evil report to their father." *Vayeshev 37:2*

9.1 That is, whatever the world does without an awareness of G•d is an aspect of evil, for "the soul without knowledge [of G•d] is not good."[100] But, Joseph would bring their evil report to their father. That is, he would bind them to their root.[101]

Degel Machane Ephraim, Vayeshev

"These are the generations of Jacob, Joseph was seventeen years old, and shepherded the flock with his brothers." *Vayeshev 37:2*

9.2 The word "shepherd" (*ro'eh*) implies "to unite, join or link together," as in the words "brotherliness" and "friendship."[102] A shepherd is called a *ro'eh* because he brings the flock together in one place, lest they become scattered. Thus, Joseph united his brothers — that is, all of Israel

---

[100] Proverbs 19:2.
[101] The Tzaddik, represented by Joseph, would uplift to his Father in Heaven all the deeds performed in the world without a consciousness of G•d.
[102] The Hebrew word ro'eh is grammatically connected to the word for "friendship" — re'ut.

VAYESHEV

and the sparks of the Divine Presence.[103] He uplifted and repaired all of them by means of the holy mystical unifications that he performed. He did this with the "flock," which implies Unifications.[104]

      Degel Machane Ephraim, Vayeshev

---

[103] The concept of mystical unifications — yichudim — is one of the central teachings of the Baal Shem Tov, and operates on many levels. The basic level is the recognition of the presence of the Creator in all aspects of creation, be they physical, emotional, conceptual, and even spiritual. Thus, the Baal Shem Tov said: "Whatever you see, remember G•d. If you feel love, remember the love of G•d. If you experience fear, recall the fear of G•d. Even when you go to the bathroom, think to yourself, I am removing the bad from the good, so that the good will remain in the service of G•d. This is the meaning of unification" (*Tzivos HaRivash, p.3b*). On a deeper level, it means the mystical recombination of the letters of creation, especially in prayer and Torah study, that can produce a revelation of the Divine Oneness in the world. In the verse above, the Baal Shem Tov is saying that Joseph, who represents the Tzaddik, is able to see the divinity in each Jew, and through this, uplift all of Israel to the Father in Heaven. Alternatively, Joseph could see the Hebrew letters that constitute all of reality, and combine them in patterns that would reveal the Divine Presence in creation.

[104] The three letters of the Hebrew word for flock, tzon, can be divided into tz — o (tzade aleph), whose numerical value is 91, and nun. The number 91 is also the numerical value (gematria) of two of G•d's holy names together — the Tetragrammaton, Y — H — V — H (26), and the name Ado — nai (65). The union of these

GENESIS

"And Joseph dreamed a dream." *Vayeshev 37:5*

9.3 Rabbi Yehoshua ben Levi said: "Come and see. G•d's traits are not like man's traits. A human being inflicts with a knife and heals with a bandage. G•d, however, heals with the very thing

---

names represents the complete integration of the spiritual and the physical, from the first emanations from G•d, until malchus, the world in which we live. (See *Likutey Moharan I:66*) The letter nun usually represents the world of Binah, which corresponds to the revelation of the world — to — come, and is the sefirah through which Divine blessing flows into the world. All this is alluded to in the word tzon — the union of G•d's two names, which leads to a subsequent outflow of blessing in the world. Thus, R. Yaakov Yosef of Polnoye writes, in the name of the Baal Shem Tov: "A human being in this world is composed of matter and form (i.e., the material and the spiritual), and through him, the lower world and the upper world are joined, and a union is created between the two names Y — H — V — H and Ado — nai, which have the numerical value of 91, from the world tzon. Whereas the effluence that pours forth from there is the expansion of the nun." (*Tzafna Paneach, Teruma*) It is also possible that the Baal Shem Tov uses the term tzon to represent this idea, because a flock is a group of animals that are joined together, and convey the idea of union. Furthermore, the word tzon is from the Hebrew word tze, which means "to go out," and represents the idea of that which emanates from a source. (See *Torah Ohr*, by the *Ba'al HaTanya, VaYetze*, p. 23c, who discusses this idea).

VAYESHEV

with which He inflicts, as it says: 'For I will restore to you your health, and I will heal you from your wounds."[105] (*Jeremiah 30:17*) Joseph was sold because of a dream . . . . . and he ruled because of a dream.[106]

On the verse: "It is a time of distress for Jacob, and from it he will be delivered," (*Jeremiah 30:7*) the Baal Shem Tov commented: From the Harsh Judgments themselves sprout forth the deliverance.

Beis Yisroel Zidichov, Vayetze

And his father guarded the matter. *Vayeshev 37:11*

9.4 Thought precedes speech, and gives birth to it. Thus, thought is called "father," and speech is called "offspring.""His father guarded the matter" means that thought guards speech, so that a person only speaks that which is appropriate.

Megadim, Mishpatim

---

[105] The implication being that G•d heals with the wound itself.
[106] *Midrash Tanchuma*, Vayeshev 9.

GENESIS

"And he said, I am seeking my brothers . . . . ."
Vayeshev 37:16

The Zohar says: Rabbi Yehuda commented on the verse: "O, were you like my brother, who nursed from the breasts of my mother. When I would find you outside, I would kiss you." *Song of Songs 8:1.* I would find You outside — meaning, in the exile, in other lands."[107]

9.5 In this piece of Zohar, one can find the words of the Baal Shem Tov, that in the Diaspora, special help is available to a person seeking Divine inspiration,[108] despite the fact that the Shechina does not dwell in exile.[109] Even if a person is not entirely worthy, heaven is still not so particular with him, as in the Land of Israel. For when a king is on the road, he must sleep in inns and hotels that are not as clean and beautiful as befitting his honor; yet, the king is not disgraced, because everyone knows that he is traveling. Understand this well.[110] *Irga d' Pirka 148*

---

[107] *Zohar I:184a*, on *Genesis 37:16*.
[108] Ruach HaKodesh.
[109] *Zohar II: 5a, 82a*.
[110] The Baal Shem Tov means that because the Divine Presence is in exile in the world, and no longer focused

VAYESHEV

"When Judah saw her [Tamar], he thought that she was a harlot, because she had covered her face." *Vayeshev 38:15*

9.6 Our Sages said that Tamar covered her face while in her father — in — law's house.[111] When the

---

in the land of Israel and the Holy Temple, it is actually easier to come to a perception of G•d than in the past. On this idea, Rabbi Yaakov Yosef of Polnoye writes (*Toldot Yaakov Yosef, Ekev, 181b*): "Especially in our time, when the Divine Presence is in exile and finds no place to rest, as soon as a person prepares all of his actions for the sake of heaven, he immediately becomes a "throne" for the Shechina, which rests upon him. He is even considered higher than those of earlier generations, when there were many Tzaddikim in the world; whereas today, "the pious man ceases" (*Psalms 12:2*) — that is, those who are pious before their Creator (*Zohar III: 281b*). A person should strengthen himself like a warrior, and show kindness to the Shechina, so that he becomes a throne for the attribute of Loving Kindness (Chesed). Just as in Abraham's time, when there was no one to help the Shechina but him, now too, besides a very few individuals, no one thinks about how to help and support the Shechina in this bitter exile. Thus, a person who is willing to sacrifice will certainly become a throne for the Divine Presence with the trait of loving kindness."

[111] *Sotah 10a*. Tamar was exceedingly modest while in Yehuda's house, and constantly covered her face with a veil. Thus, when she pretended to be a harlot, she merely had to uncover her face to deceive him.

GENESIS

Baal Shem Tov was in Istanbul,[112] he saw young Torah scholars who had the souls of Tannaim,[113] due to the great modesty of the women there.[114]
Midrash Pinchas HaChadash 28

"And it came to pass, as she spoke to Joseph day by day, that he did not listen to her, to lie with her, or to be with her. And it came to pass, about this time, that Joseph went into the house to do his work, and there was none of the men in the house within. And she caught him by his garment and said, Like with me; and he left his garment in her hand, and fled and went outside." *Vayeshev 39:10,12*

---

[112] During his aborted trip to the Land of Israel.

[113] The Tannaim were the Sages of the Land of Israel from the first to third centuries, such as Rabbi Akiva, Rabbi Eliezer the Great, Rabbi Yishmael, and whose statements comprise the Mishnah. They were among the greatest souls in Jewish history.

[114] This is based upon the principle that modesty, both on the part of men and women, enables a couple to bring down holy souls to their children. The Talmud tells the story of Kimchit, who would cover her hair even in her house, and who deserved to have seven sons who served as High Priests in the Temple in Jerusalem. From Tamar, as well, came the King David, and eventually, the Messiah.

VAYESHEV

9.7 Sages have explained that when Potiphar's wife tried to seduce Joseph, he saw an image of his father, Jacob.[115] It is known that Potiphar's wife would make herself look extremely beautiful to Joseph.[116] "The clothing she wore in the morning, she would not wear in the afternoon, and that what she wore in the afternoon, she would change in the evening" — all in order to seduce him. Joseph did not want this beauty; however, by means of this beauty, he desired and was burned for the Supernal Beauty, which was [represented by] the image of his father — *Tiferet Yisroel*.[117] This is what it means, "he fled and went outside." He fled from the physical beauty and was inspired to run out beyond this world, to cleave to the Supernal Beauty.

Torah Ohr, VaYetze

---

[115] *Sotah 36b.*

[116] *Midrash Tanchuma, Vayeshev 5.*

[117] A phrase meaning the beauty, or glory, of Israel. Here, the Baal Shem Tov applies it to Jacob — Israel. According to Kabbalah, Jacob corresponds to the sefirah of Tiferet, which means beauty or resplendence. Joseph was not satisfied by physical beauty, for he saw it as only a lower manifestation, of spiritual beauty. This principle can be applied to all things in the world. (See footnote 103, above.) Although the wife of Potiphar tried to seduce him with physical beauty, he saw in it a reflection of Tiferet, the supernal source of beauty, represented by his father Jacob.

GENESIS

"And Pharaoh said to Joseph: 'I have dreamt a dream, and there is no one who can interpret it.'" *Vayeshev 41:15*

9.8 In order to annul a bad dream, immerse yourself in a mikvah, and unite the three [Divine] Names that are within the Name "Yabok" (יבק).[118] Do this is as follows: The floor of the mikvah is *Ad'nus*.[119] The person himself is *Havayeh*.[120] And the water that covers his head, wherein is his consciousness, is *Ekiyeh*.[121] These have the combined numerical value of 112.[122] You should also meditate on אלד, which has the numerical value of אגלא, interspersed in its source Ekiyeh, like this: אאהלידה.

This is good to do on Rosh Hashanah and on Hoshanah Rabbah.

The Siddur of R. Shabsai, p. 44

---

[118] The Name Yabok has the numerical value of the three Divine Names, Ad'nus (65), Y — H — V — H (26), and Ekiyeh (21). These correspond to the Sefiros of Malchus, Tiferes, and Kesser, respectively.
[119] G•d's name spelled Ado — nai is read as Adnus, so as not to unnecessarily pronounce the Name
[120] I.e., the Tetragrammaton.
[121] From *Exodus 3:14:* "I will be what I will be." Read as "Ekiyeh."
[122] Equal to the Name Yabok, יבק — קיב.

CHAPTER TEN

MIKETZ

GENESIS

"And it came to pass, at the end of two years . . ." Miketz 41:1

"He makes an end to darkness" (Job 28:3). A limit was set as to how long the world will remain in darkness. For as long as the evil inclination is in the world, there is darkness and distress; when the evil inclination is removed from the world, there will be no more darkness and distress.

Midrash Rabbah, Miketz 89:1

10.1 The mystical writings of the Arizal[123] explain the concept of the extraction of the holy sparks, that fell in the time of the breakage [of the vessels], and how a person must raise these sparks from the level of mineral to vegetable, animal and speaker.[124]

---

[123] Rabbi Yitzchak Luria (1534 — 1572), one of the most influential kabbalists in history, known also as the Arizal, the "Lion," of blessed memory.

[124] According to the Arizal, as a consequence of the primordial breaking of the vessels, and the subsequent sin of Adam, sparks of holiness became dispersed in all things in this world, on all levels of existence: mineral, vegetable, animal, and even human. On the one hand, the food chain produces a natural process of elevation, as plants grow from the ground, animals eat them, and man eats animal. However, human beings also elevate the sparks in the mineral and vegetable kingdoms by

MIKETZ

Extracting these sparks of holiness from among the "shells"[125] is the purpose of all a Jews actions, in Torah study, fulfillment of the commandments, and in the mystical intentions of eating.

Each spark found within these lower levels of existence has a complete form,[126] with 248

---

consuming them directly, or making use of them in other ways.

The Baal Shem Tov's list also includes "speakers," that is, human beings; for while all people can participate in the process of uplifting sparks, not all actually do so. It depends upon how a person uses his life. One who puts the strength he receives from eating into the service of G•d uplifts the sparks that were in the food. However, a person who eats for physical gratification, and does not invest his energy into good deeds, merely traps the sparks in a further level of corporeality. However, if this person helps another person fulfill a mitzvah (for instance, a gentile worker in a Jewish religious institution), then the sparks are uplifted from him as well, and the Divine Presence is reconstituted in the world.

[125] *Kelipot*, the lower realms of reality that cover and conceal the essence of the Divine, as a shell covers a fruit.

[126] Literally, a "full stature," *komah shleimah*. Just as a human being has limbs and organs that are arranged according to a certain pattern, with the preeminent organ being the head, and moving from there down to the feet, so each holy spark also has a complete spiritual stature. Rabbi Nachman of Breslov speaks about each Torah commandment also as having a *komah shleimah*, with the "feet" of the commandment represents its

GENESIS

[spiritual] organs and 365 sinews.[127] However, as long as it is on that level, it is imprisoned, with its head is on its knees and belly,[128] unable to extend its hands and feet. A person who has good thoughts and intentions, can uplift the spark of holiness from these levels and bring them out to freedom.[129] This is the greatest fulfillment of the mitzvah of redeeming captives. And since it is the king's son himself who is in captivity, a person works to free him from his imprisonment will certainly receive

---

lowest aspect; the part of the commandment whose details are least observed, or least fulfilled with enthusiasm.

[127] The Talmud sets the number of human limbs and organs at 613 (the same as the number of Biblical commandments). These are referred to as the 248 organs and 365 sinews.

[128] As long as the spark of holiness, whose source is the human being himself, is trapped within the non — human world, it cannot express itself fully in the service of G•d. The Baal Shem Tov uses the image of a fetus, doubled over, with its head on its knees. Only when this spark is incorporated in a human being, who serves G•d, can it attain its realized state.

[129] This is also the meaning of the Pascal lamb, that was roasted with its head upon its stomach, in fetal position, to symbolize the slavery of the Jewish people in Egypt, who were not able to achieve their full stature as servants of G•d, until the exodus. On this, see *Derech Mitzvosecha, mitzvah Korban Pesach*, by the Tzemach Tzedek of Lubavitch.

MIKETZ

abundant reward. Nevertheless, everything follows the supernal judgment that has set an end to darkness, and has determined just how long something will remain imprisoned, when it will deserve to exit, and through whom it will attain freedom.

Ben Poras Yosef, p. 74b

10.2 "Happy is the man who makes G•d his trust . . . . ." *Psalms 40:5*. This refers to Joseph.[130] The verse says, "Blessed is the man who trusts in G•d, and G•d will be his trust" *Jeremiah 17:7*. The Baal Shem Tov taught, there is the one who trusts, the one who promises, and the thing that is trusted in; that is, the agent upon which a person relies to receive the promise. For instance, G•d promises to provide a person with all of his needs, if he follows His ways, and the person trusts in this. However, he still needs some causal agent by means of which G•d will send him his livelihood, such as a business deal, or other transaction.

Such a person has not reached the essence of faith. Because the main thing is to believe in G•d alone, and nothing else. A person with faith does not need any intermediary agents through which to

---

[130] *Pesikta Rabbosai*, 89:3.

attain his livelihood. G•d is the ultimate cause and mover of all. Even if he makes *no* efforts to support himself, G•d can still send him his livelihood, in His great love. This is the meaning of: "Blessed is the man who trusts in G•d, and G•d will be his trust." That is, our trust is G•d Himself, for He alone is the source of our livelihood. Everything is only G•d, may He be blessed. Even if a person receives support through intermediary means, he must believe fully that it is only from G•d, who wants to support him this way, though it does not necessarily have to come through this channel. Only trust in G•d. This is a very high level.

Degel Machane Ephraim, BeShalach

10.3 And there came a man from Ba'al shalisha, and brought the man of G•d bread of the first fruits, twenty loaves of barley, and full ears of corn in his sack. And he [Elisha] said, "Give to the people, that they may eat. And his attendant said, "What, should I set this before a hundred men?" He said again, "Give the people that they may eat: for thus says the L•rd, They shall eat, and shall leave over. So he set it before them, and they did eat, and left some of it over, according to the word of the L•rd.

II Kings 4:42, 44

MIKETZ

10.4 The Baal Shem Tov said that his trust in G•d was so complete that he could feed the entire world, the problem was that he had no one to cook for him.

My father [R. Yehezkel of Kozhmir] explained his holy words as follows. Elisha the Prophet said to his servant, Gehazi, "Give to the people that they may eat." Gehazi asked, "Is this enough for a hundred men?" Didn't Elisha know how many students he had? Of course he did. However, Gehazi in his incredulity and skepticism ruined Elisha's intention, and he had to tell him a second time: "Thus says the L•rd . . ."

Divrei Yisroel

"He will do the desire of those who fear Him, He will hear their cry and deliver them." *Psalms 145:19.*

10.5 Really, those who truly fear G•d have no desire of their own. Their trust and faith in Him is so great that they say "Whatever the Compassionate One does is for the good."[131] They known that G•d desires their welfare more than they could ever ask

---

[131] *Berachos* 60b.

for themselves. However, the Holy One longs for the prayers of His righteous,[132] and creates in them desire, that they should pray to Him, and He can fulfill their prayers. Thus, the verse says, "He makes the desire of those who fear Him,"[133] in order that "He will hear their cry and deliver them."

Tefilah l'Moshe, Tehilim

"Happy is the man who makes G•d his trust, and does not turn to the arrogant" *Psalms 40:5.*

10.6 This is Joseph. [However,] by saying to the wine steward, "remember me," and "mention me to Pharaoh" two years were added [to his sentence].[134]

The verse says: "Blessed is the man who trusts in G•d, and G•d will be his trust" (*Jeremiah 17:7*). You should not trust in G•d to provide you with a lot of food and material goods, for perhaps He will not. Rather, when you serve Him, you can trust that He will send you a mitzvah, and surely give you the strength to fulfill it. Don't rely on food for this strength; just trust simply that G•d will give

---

[132] *Yevamos* 64a.
[133] The Hebrew word *aseh* can mean both "make" and "do."
[134] *Midrash Rabbah, Bereishit* 89:3.

it to you. For G•d is not limited to food to deliver a person. This is the meaning of "and G•d will be his trust" — and not by eating.

Kisvei Kodesh, p. 18b

10.7 Your thoughts should be above in the Supernal World when you serve G•d. Cling to Him and trust in Him that you will achieve your goal.

Tzava'as HaRivash, p. 4a

10.8 The great principle in life is: "Commit you actions to G•d, and your thoughts will be established" *Proverbs 16:3*. Whatever comes to you, imagine that it is from G•d. Ask G•d to always give you what He knows is best for you, and not what seems [good] to human intellect. Because what might seem good in your eyes may be bad in His. Rather, throw everything — all your concerns and needs — upon G•d.

Tzava'as HaRivash, p. 2a

10.9 Keep in mind always that the entire world is filled with the Creator, may He be blessed, as it is written: "Do I not fill heaven and earth? says G•d" (*Jeremiah 23:24*). Realize that even what happens as a result of human thought and planning is from G•d. Even the most insignificant event in the world is under His guidance. When a person realizes this, it makes no difference to him if his actions come out as he desires or not, since everything is from G•d, who knows that it is better for a person's will not be done. In light of this, a person should never despair when something he wants to do does not succeed, for he believes that G•d desires the opposite. [He should think:] "If it were good in G•d's eyes, He certainly would help me achieve it. But since I am can't, it certainly is not according to G•d's will. In fact, G•d was much kinder to me than had He fulfilled my will.

Hanhagos Yesharos, p. 10a

CHAPTER 11

VAYIGASH

GENESIS

"And Judah drew near to him (Yosef) and said, 'Oh my lord!'" *Vayigash 44:18*

11.1 The Talmud says, "A person should always praise G•d first, and then pray [for his needs].[135] Yet, in another place, the Talmud states the opposite view.[136] The answer is that there are two separate opinions. The Ramban[137] writes that the essence of a craftsman can be found in the craft that he creates.[138] [Likewise], the Creation is compared to a snail, whose garment is part of itself.[139] In all suffering, there exists a spark of holiness from G•d, although it is hidden within many garments. This is the meaning of the verse: "the seven maids chosen to be given to her, from the king's house"[140] (*Esther 2:9*). When a

---

[135] Berachos 31a.
[136] "Rabbi Eliezer said, a person should first ask for his needs, and then pray." Avoda Zara 7b.
[137] Nachmanidies (1194 — 1270).
[138] Meaning, whenever a person creates something, something of his soul enters into and remains in their handicraft. Great kabbalists, such as the Arizal and the Baal Shem Tov could look at an object, and immediately know everything about the one who made it. Here, the Baal Shem Tov applies the principle to creation itself. Since it is G•d's handiwork, there must be a remnant of the Creator within it.
[139] Midrash Rabbosai, Bereishit 21:5. Just as the garments of a locust are part of itself, so the creation is not something separate from or outside of the Divine. It is part of Him, and His Presence is continually present within it.
[140] The "seven maids" represent the sparks of holiness that have fallen among the "shells" of impurity. The word maid, na'arah, is related to the word "to shake out," mino'ar, because the holiness found in these sparks has been "shaken out" of

VAYIGASH

person realizes that G•d is with him even there, the garments become transparent and disappear, and the suffering is abated.

This is what it means to offer praise first. G•d's praise is that His glory fills the entire universe. "In all their afflictions, He is afflicted" (*Isaiah 63:9*) — then, there is *no* affliction[141] — and one can pray. When one knows how to praise G•d in this way, the suffering will disappear by itself.[142]

The other opinion says to pray first.[143] In this case, a person's has faith that G•d is also there [in the affliction], so that he can offer his praise [afterward].[144]

---

them, until almost nothing remains. However, these sparks yearn to return to their root. Thus, the verse from Esther continues: "When it came the turn for each maid to come into the king..." (Esther 2:12); that is, each spark of holiness has a predetermined time that it will leave the shells of impurity, and come before the King. (See Baal Shem Tov on the Torah, Miketz, on Genesis 41:1.

[141] The word lo in this verse is written different than it is read. It is written lamed vav, which mean "him," in this case, G•d. However, tradition tells us to read the word lo as though it were written with lamed aleph, which means "no," in this case, "there is not." The Baal Shem Tov combines both readings. When a person realizes that G•d is present in all of his afflictions, then the afflictions themselves cease to exist.

[142] R. Yaakov Yosef adds here: "I heard from my Master (the Baal Shem Tov) that this is the meaning of 'You will establish their heart, Your ears will hear [their prayers]" (Psalms 10:17).

[143] I.e., a person who prays for his needs, without first praising G•d; that is, coming to the realization that G•d is present even in the affliction.

GENESIS

With this, we can understand the verse: "And Judah drew near to him."[145] He praised the Holy One.[146] First, he said, "Oh my L•rd" — because all affliction derives from this name.[147] But when he drew near to Him and praised and exalted Him, the affliction was annulled.[148]

Toldot Yaakov Yosef, Vayechi

---

[144] In other words, even though a person does not perceive the spark of holiness in the suffering, if he believes that G•d is with him even there, he will eventually come to this realization.
[145] The Baal Shem Tov reads Judah's words as not being addressed to Joseph, but to G•d himself. See Pri Tzaddik, Vayigash 1, by Rabbi Tzaddok HaKohen of Lublin, who explains that tzaddikim often address their words to the Divine Presence, even when they are speaking to other human beings.
[146] The name Judah — Yehuda — is from the Hebrew word "hodu" — to praise. As Leah said, when he was born: "Now I will praise G•d; therefore, she called his name Judah" (Genesis 29:35). And Jacob said: "Judah, your brothers will praise you" (ibid. 49:8).
[147] The Hebrew reads: "Bi Adoni." The Baal Shem Tov sees this as alluding to G•d's name Ado — nai, which represents the forces of concealment and strict judgment.
[148] I.e., Joseph revealed himself. Then, the very source of the their problem — the evil viceroy of Egypt — turned out to be their beloved brother, whose intentions were only for their good.

CHAPTER 12

VAYECHI

GENESIS

"And Jacob called to his sons and said, Gather yourselves together, that I may tell you what will happen to you in the end of days." *Vayechi 49:1*

12.1 Jacob said, "What will happen" — because the redemption will seem to just happen.[149] Everyone will be busy with their work, not thinking about it at all, and suddenly, the Messiah will come.

Yalkut Moshe, Vayechi

12.2 The Baal Shem Tov said that in the process of the Messiah's coming, no one will have to die, G•d forbid

Midrash Pinchas, p. 28

"Yissachar is a strong ass, crouching down between the sheep folds." *Vayechi 49:14*

12.3 That is, [spiritual] reward[150] can be brought forth from the material world.[151] By eating and drinking, for

---

[149] The word *mikreh* in Hebrew means "an occurrence," and has the implication of a chance happening.

[150] The name Yissachar can be divided into two words, *yesh sachar* — "there is reward." The very name Yissachar is related to this idea, as Leah said when she named him: "G•d has given me my reward, because I gave my handmaid to my husband" (Genesis 30:18).

[151] The hebrew word for donkey, *chamor*, is related to the word for material substance, *chomer*, and the word for "strong," in this verse *gorem*, also has the meaning of "to cause" or "bring about."

instance, we uplift the sparks of holiness[152] that were "crouching down" amidst the different elements of the physical world, and in the low places.

Ohr HaGanuz LaTzaddikim, Vayechi

12.4 The Talmud says: "The Torah is careful with a Jew's money."[153] Why? Because in everything a Jew uses, be it clothing, food, or utensils, there is a spiritual life—force from which he derives pleasure. Without this energy, the object could not exist. Furthermore, these sparks of holiness are connected to the person's own soul, which explains why one person loves one thing, and another person hates it, and loves something else. And even when a person uses the object, or eats the food, just to sustain himself, he can still repairs its sparks, if he later serves G•d with the strength that he received from it. This explains why sometimes, after a person has repaired the sparks in a object related to his soul, G•d removes it from him and gives it to someone else, because it still contains other sparks from a different source.

The Baal Shem Tov said: "We eat people, we drink people, and we use people" — referring to the sparks that are in each thing.[154] Therefore, we should be careful with

---

[152] The idea that the physical world contains sparks of holiness was discussed in previous week lessons.
[153] *Rosh Hashana* 27a.
[154] Rabbi Chaim of Chernovitz, in the famous Chassidic work *Be'er Mayim Chayim* (commentary on the Hagada), gives a slightly different interpretation of these words: "The Baal Shem

our possessions, because of the sparks that they contain. We should have compassion on our own sparks of holiness.

Tzivos HaRivash, p.13a

"And [Jacob] expired, and was gathered to his people."
Vayechi 49:33

12.5 The Torah never says that Jacob died.[155] Likewise, the Sages said: "Our father Jacob did not die."[156] I heard from my grandfather (the Baal Shem Tov) that the Torah is called "Jacob." Just as Jacob did not die, so the Torah is eternal, and will never disappear.

Degel Machane Ephraim, Vayigash

Tov said, 'Three people who eat together, and do not share word of Torah, are considered to have eaten from the sacrifices of the dead' (Pirkei Avos 3:4). This refers to the souls of the deceased that are incarnated in human food, so that people will share words of Torah over them. Through this 'the dead are resurrected' (i.e. repaired). However, if they do not share Torah, it is as if they sacrificed that soul and threw it down to the level of inanimate objects."

[155] See Rashi on this verse.
[156] *Ta'anis* 5b.

CHAPTER 13

SHEMOT

EXODUS

"Now these are the names of the sons of Israel who came to Egypt with Jacob; every man with his family: Reuben, Simeon, Levi, and Judah . ."

Shemot 1:1,2

13.1 When a person experiences fear of G•d, or a sense of satisfaction in performing a commandment, he begins to feel self important. This brings exile into the world. Thus, the verse says: ". . . . they have made Jerusalem (*Yerushalayim*) into heaps." (*Psalms 79:1*) That is, they made their perfect fear (*yira — shalem*) into a high and impressive mound. When he serves G•d, whether in prayer, Torah study or the like, it is without fear and love, but like someone strumming on a harp. And so, all of his worship goes to the *kelipos*. Thus it says: "They have given the corpses (*nivlas*) of Your servants as food to the birds of the heaven." (ibid. 79:2) These are the *kelipos*. And what caused this? Because they performed their service as if on a harp (*nevel*).

This may be hinted to in the verse above: "These are the names (*Shemot*)." That is, what caused the exile and destruction (*shemomon*), and

SHEMOT

brought them to Egypt — to the straits of exile?[157] The answer is: "Reuben" — when a person serves G•d and says "See the difference (*re'u bein*) between me and other people! My service of G•d is perfect. G•d should hear my voice and accompany me." This is "Simeon, Levi."[158]

This applies to the other names, as well.

Tzava'as HaRivash, p. 15b[159]

"Reuben, Simeon, Levi, Judah, Issachar, Zevulun . . . . ." *Shemot 1:1,2*

13.2 Just as the names of the tribes exist on the side holiness, so they exist in the *kelipos*.[160]

---

[157] The word Egypt — *Mitzrayim* — is related to the word *metzer* — a place of constriction.
[158] From the words *shimo'ah*, "to hear," and *"levi,"* to accompany, as in: "And [Leah] conceived again, and bore a son; and said: 'Because G•d has heard (*shoma*) that I am hated, He has given me this son also.' And she called his name Simeon (Shimon). And she conceived again, and bore a son; and said: 'Now my husband will be joined to me (*yiloveh*), because I have born him three sons.' Therefore his name was called Levi" (*Genesis 29:33, 34*).
[159] See, also *Ohr Torah, Shemot*.
[160] The realm of evil.

EXODUS

Reuben — "See (*re'u*) that I am a son (*ben*)."[161]

Simeon — he does good in order for his fame[162] to spread throughout the land.

Levi — he attaches himself to righteous individuals.

Yehuda — in order that they will praise him.[163]

Then he will be in a Issachar — Zebulun relationship — he will study Torah and they will support him.

Toldot Yaakov Yosef, p. 150d with *Ben Poras Yosef*, p. 5d

13.3 Just as the entire nation of Israel experiences exile and redemption, so does each and every individual, as the verse says: "Draw near to my soul and redeem it" (*Psalms 69:19*). Therefore, a person should first pray for the redemption of his soul, before praying for the redemption of the nation.

Toldot Yaakov Yosef, Shemini

---

[161] I.e., "See that I am a Tzaddik, a beloved son of G•d."
[162] "*Sham'u*" — from "Shimon."
[163] *Yodu*, from the name Yehuda.

13.4 There are two types of exile: one is the physical exile of the nation, and the other is the spiritual exile in the evil inclination — the exile of the soul. And one follows from the other.

Toldot Yaakov Yosef, p. 175b

"And He said, I am the G•d of your father."
Shemot 3:6

13.5 This is what is written: "A fool (*pesi*) believes in everything" (*Proverbs 14:15*). What is the meaning of "a fool"? A child. Because in Arabia, they call a child a *pasia*.

Midrash Rabbah, Shemot 3

13.6 The Baal Shem Tov told his students: "Despite the profound levels of understanding that I attained in the [supernal] roots of the Torah and the mitzvos, and despite all the spiritual ecstasy that I experienced, I put everything aside to serve G•d in simple faith. I am a fool and believe — *Ich bin a naar un gleib!*[164] And even though it is written: "A

---

[164] The Baal Shem Tov is making a word — play on the statement of the Midrash, above. The Hebrew word for child, *na'ar*, is similar to the Yiddish word for fool.

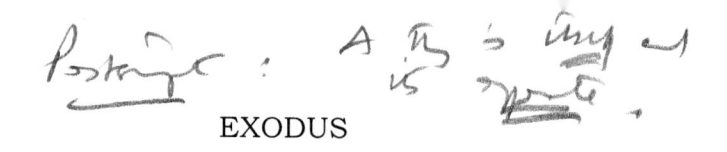

fool believes in everything," it is also written: "G•d protects the fools." (Psalms 116:6).

"And I have come down to deliver them out of the hand of the Egyptians, and to bring them up out of that land to a good and broad land, a land flowing with milk and honey; to the place of the Canaanite, and the Hittite, and the Amorite, and the Perizzite, and the Hivite, and the Jebusite."
Shemot 3:8

13.7 The seven nations that inhabited the Land of Israel stand in direct opposition to the seven attributes.[165] For instance, opposite the love of G•d are the Canaanites, who represent the love of other things. Opposite fear of G•d,[166] are the Hittites.[167] This is true of them all. And since love should be only for G•d, and for those whom G•d wishes to

---

[165] I.e., the seven traits that are associated with the seven lower sefirot: Chesed — love, Gevurah — fear, Tiferet — balance, etc.
[166] Literally, "*pachad Yitzchak*" — the fear of Isaac. A reference to G•d, from *Genesis 31:42*.
[167] The word *Hittite* relates to the Hebrew *hit*, which means "to be terrified."

SHEMOT

make beloved, the land is called the "Land of the Canaanites."[168]

Zos Zicharon, Emor

13.8 If you feel the desire to commit a sin, recite the Torah verses that speak of that sin, with its syllables and cantillation marks, in fear and love of G•d, and the desire will pass. And if you feel overwhelmed by some bad trait, say the names of the six nations:[169] the Canaanites, etc., with

---

[168] Apparently, the Baal Shem Tov means that the intrinsic nature of the Land of Israel is the love of G•d; thus it is called the Land of Canaan. However, before the Jewish people took possession of the land, this love was distorted into love of other things (materialism, licentiousness, etc.). With the Jewish people's presence in the land, this trait was uplifted. Rabbi Nathan of Breslov, in *Likutey Halachot, Milah 3:5*, writes that the seven Canaanite nations that inhabited the Land of Israel correspond to the seven days that a Jewish male child must pass through until his circumcision on the eight day. Cutting off the foreskin, which symbolizes the forces of concealment and animalism, is similar to the defeat of the seven nations, and the uplifting of love to its Divine source.

[169] It is not clear whether the Baal Shem Tov means the six nations mentioned in this verse, or in the verse from *Nechemiah 9:8*: "You found his heart faithful before You, and made a covenant with him to give the land of the Canaanite, the Hittite, the Amorite, and the Perizzite, and the Jebusite, and the Girgashite, even to give it to

EXODUS

absolute concentration, in fear and love, and the bad trait will pass.

Tzivos HaRivash, p.3a

"And G•d spoke unto Moses, and said unto him: 'I am the L•rd; and I appeared to Abraham, to Isaac, and to Jacob, as G•d Almighty, but My Name YHWH — I was not known to them.'"
Shemot 6:2

13.9 G•d and His Name are one, unlike His creatures, whose names and essence are distinct. It would be incorrect for the verse to say "My Name YHWH, I did not make known to them," because the Name itself is speaking.[170] Therefore, the verse must say, "I was not known to them."

---

his seed." R. Elimelech of Lizensk, in the *Tzetel Katan* (the "Small Letter"), writes that a person should say the names of all seven nations.

[170] I.e., there is a discrepancy in the use of the verb "to know" in this verse. Since G•d is speaking about something He did, it should say, "but My Name YHWH, I did not make known to them"; however, it says, "I was not known to them."

SHEMOT

These are the words of the Ohr HaChaim,[171] and I also heard them from my grandfather [the Baal Shem Tov], in the name of the *Chovas HaLevavos*.[172]

Degel Machane Ephraim, Terumah

"And I will take you to Me for a people, and I will be to you a G•d; and you shall know that I am the L•rd your G•d, who brought you out from under the burdens of the Egyptians." *Shemot 6:70*

This commandment precedes all the other commandments; for the first commandment is to know G•d, in general, and in particular.[173] *Zohar 2:25a*

13.10 The verse says: "Know the G•d of your fathers" (*I Chronicles 28:9*). That is, the ultimate

---

[171] The great Sefardic Sage (1696 — 1743). See his commentary on this verse.
[172] *Duties of the Heart* — a famous Twelfth Century philosophical work, by R. Bachya ibn Paquda. However, this teaching is not found in the edition of the book we have today.
[173] I.e., to know that G•d exists and rules over all creation, and to know him personally, in one's life.

knowledge is to realize that everything that happens to us in life, and in the world around us, is from G•d. Though this concept is extremely deep, and impossible to explain, there is still a little we can say about it.

A person who has wealth, honor, and blessing in his life, should realize that they come from the side of *Chesed* (Loving kindness) that is in the Shechina.[174] Because each human being is a "limb" of the Shechina, and the entire world together constitutes its complete form. Likewise, a person who suffers poverty and affliction, G•d forbid, is experiencing the trait of *Gevurah* (severity) in the Shechina. And from that place, he must pray to G•d. This is the meaning of the verse: "With this, shall Aharon come into the holy place" (*Leviticus 16:3*).[175] If he feels that both traits are present in his life, he should realize that they derive from the trait of Tiferet (Harmony). This applies to all traits.

A person who one day finds himself unable to serve G•d, should realize that this too is in the

---

[174] The Divine Presence that is found within creation.
[175] That is, nothing is accidental. If a person is in a low place, it is because G•d wants him to pray to Him from there, and lift up the low level to its root in holiness. According to the Zohar, the word "this," *zos*, refers to the Shechina.

SHEMOT

Shechina, and is called "First Smallness," or "Second Smallness."[176] Everything a person experiences or feels is in the Shechina, and he has to know how to unite that trait with the corresponding trait Above.

This is true in general, and in particular; for there are myriads of details in which this applies. A perfected human being can unite the Holy One and the Shechina with every step.[177] Everything he does, including physical actions, his food, his job, can be united and reflect to him the corresponding trait in the Shechina.

---

[176] The Baal Shem Tov is referring to movements in the sefirotic realm. When the various lower sefirot receive illumination from their higher sources, they are in a state of Largeness, *Gadlus*. When this illumination is cut off, often as part of the process of sefirotic development, they are in a state of Smallness, *Katnus*. There are several stages in this process, including First Smallness and Second Smallness. The Baal Shem Tov is applying these states to the human mind.

[177] The union of the Holy One and the Shechina is the goal of all Kabbalistic practice, and means the complete unity of all elements of creation, to bring about a revelation of G•d in the world. See *The Path of the Just*, by R. Moshe Chaim Luzzato, chapter 26, for a beautiful discussion of this point.

EXODUS

This is the meaning of the verse: "Know the G•d of your fathers," and also, the meaning of the quote from the Zohar above.

Understand this![178]

---

[178] *Degel Machane Ephraim, Va'eschanan*

CHAPTER 14

VAYERA

"And G•d spoke unto Moses, and said unto him: 'I am the L•rd; and I appeared to Abraham, to Isaac, and to Jacob, as G•d Almighty, but My Name YHWH — I was not known to them."
Vayera 6:2

14.1 G•d and His Name are one, unlike His creatures, whose names and essence are distinct. It would be incorrect for the verse to say "My Name YHWH, I did not make known to them," because the Name itself is speaking.[179] Therefore, the verse must say, "I was not known to them."

These are the words of the Ohr HaChaim,[180] and I also heard them from my grandfather [the Baal Shem Tov], in the name of the *Chovas HaLevavos*.[181]

Degel Machane Ephraim, Terumah

---

[179] I.e., there is a discrepancy in the use of the verb "to know" in this verse. Since G•d is speaking about something He did, it should say, "but My Name YHWH, I did not make known to them"; however, it says, "I was not known to them."

[180] The great Sefardic Sage (1696 —1743). See his commentary on this verse.

[181] *Duties of the Heart* — a famous Twelfth Century philosophical work, by R. Bachya ibn Paquda. However, this teaching is not found in the edition of the book we have today.

VAYERA

"And I will take you to Me for a people, and I will be to you a G•d; and you shall know that I am the L•rd your G•d, who brought you out from under the burdens of the Egyptians." *Vayera 6:70*

This commandment precedes all the other commandments; for the first commandment is to know G•d, in general, and in particular.[182]

Zohar 2:25a.

14.2 The verse says: "Know the G•d of your fathers" (*I Chronicles 28:9*). That is, the ultimate knowledge is to realize that everything that happens to us in life, and in the world around us, is from G•d. Though this concept is extremely deep, and impossible to explain, there is still a little we can say about it.

A person who has wealth, honor, and blessing in his life, should realize that they come from the side of *Chesed* (Loving kindness) that is in the Shechina.[183] Because each human being is a "limb" of the Shechina, and the entire world

---

[182] I.e., to know that G•d exists and rules over all creation, and to know him personally, in one's life.
[183] The Divine Presence that is found within creation.

EXODUS

together constitutes its complete form. Likewise, a person who suffers poverty and affliction, G•d forbid, is experiencing the trait of *Gevurah* (Severity) in the Shechina. And from that place, he must pray to G•d. This is the meaning of the verse: "With this, shall Aharon come into the holy place" (Leviticus 16:3).[184] If he feels that both traits are present in his life, he should realize that they derive from the trait of *Tiferet* (Harmony). This applies to all traits.

A person who one day finds himself unable to serve G•d, should realize that this too is in the Shechina, and is called "First Smallness," or "Second Smallness."[185] Everything a person feels or experiences is in the Shechina, and he has to know

---

[184] That is, nothing is accidental. If a person is in a low place, it is because G•d wants him to pray to Him from there, and lift up the low level to its root in holiness. According to the Zohar, the word "this," *zos*, refers to the Shechina.

[185] The Baal Shem Tov is referring to movements in the sefirotic realm. When the various lower sefirot receive illumination from their higher sources, they are in a state of Largeness, *Gadlus*. When this illumination is cut off, often as part of the process of sefirotic development, they are in a state of Smallness, *Katnus*. There are several stages in this process, including First Smallness and Second Smallness. The Baal Shem Tov is applying these states to the human mind.

VAYERA

how to unite that trait with the corresponding trait Above.

This is true in general, and in particular; for there are myriads of details in which this applies. A perfected human being can unite the Holy One and the Shechina with every step.[186] Everything he does, including physical actions, his food, his job, everything can be united, and reflect to him the corresponding trait in the Shechina.

This is the meaning of the verse: "Know the G•d of your fathers," and also, the meaning of the quote from the Zohar above.

Understand this!

Degel Machane Ephraim, Va'eschanan

"And he said, please my L•rd, if I have found favor in your eyes, do not pass by your servant."
Vayera 18:3,4

---

[186] The union of the Holy One and the Shechina is the goal of all kabbalistic practice, and means the complete unity of all elements of creation, to bring about a revelation of G•d in the world. See *The Path of the Just*, by R. Moshe Chaim Luzzato, chapter 26, for a beautiful discussion of this point.

EXODUS

Greater is welcoming in guests than receiving the face of the Shechinah. (*Shabbat* 127a)[187]

14.3 Even though welcoming guests sometimes wastes a person's time from Torah study, or can lead one to hear defamatory stories, it is still greater than receiving the Shechinah.

Toldot Yaakov Yosef, p. 109b

14.4 "Guest" — *Oreyach* (אורח) is *Or Chet* — the "Light of Eight" (אור ח'). Thus, Abraham received guests, for *chet* is the World to Come,[188] like a guest that comes. This is the World of Binah. Abraham was the Attribute of Kindness (*Chesed*), "the day of

---

[187] The Talmud deduces this from the use of the word L•rd in the above verse, which refers to G•d, and not one of the travelers. Abraham had been in a state of communion with G•d, but when the three travelers passed by, he asked G•d to wait while he tended to their needs.

[188] The number seven represent the completion of creation, as in the seven days of the week. The number eight (*chet*) represents one level above the creation, which is the transcendent World to Come. It also corresponds to the Sefirah of Binah, which is the eighth Sefirah when counting up from Malchus.

all days,"[189] and the light of *Chesed* that passes through all the Sefiros.[190]

Therefore, Abraham would bring the Light of *Chet*, of *Binah*, into all the Sefiros.[191] And thus, he merited the entire Torah by means of the letter *hey* added to his name.[192] For this is the World of *Binah*, from where the Torah issues forth.

Degel Machane Ephraim, "Things I heard from my Grandfather"

14.5 I received from my grandfather [an explanation] of "commencing with [the honor of] the

---

[189] See *Be'er Mayim Chayim*, on *parashas Yisro* 19:6.
[190] See the writings of the Arizal in the laws on Succah.
[191] The Sefirah of Chesed is one below the Sefirah of Binah and is the first the configuration of the lower seven Sefiros, from Chesed to Malchus. Thus, it draws from the light of Binah, which corresponds to the World to Come, and shines it into the Sefiros below.
[192] The Sages say that Abraham knew and observed the entire Torah, as the verse says: "Because Abraham hearkened to My voice, and kept My charge, My commandments, My statutes, and My laws" (*Genesis 26:5*). According to the Baal Shem Tov, this is because G•d added the letter *hey* to his name, changing it from Abram to Abraham (אברם — אברהם). The first letter *hey* in the Tetragrammaton corresponds to the Sefirah of *Binah*, which is the source of the Torah.

hosts of Torah."[193] For the guest brings Torah to the host, and according to the guest is the nature of Torah that is revealed to him.

Ibid, Va'erah

"Righteousness shall go before him, and he will set his steps on the way.' *Psalms 85:14*

14.6 This is meant as an admonition. There are some people who go to perform a mitzvah, pray, etc., and stop on the way to speak with others. Even though they fulfill the mitzvah afterward, they sinned in that they did not do so quickly. After their death, their punishment is reciprocal, as is known from numerous books. Their soul is made to pass over a river on a very narrow crossing. This is a very painful to the soul, and causes it fear and dread. It must run very fast to get across. However, in the middle of the way, G•d sends an angel to obstruct it. This is the same angel that was created

---

[193] *Berachos* 83b. The Talmud relates that when the Sages reassembled in the town of Yavneh, after the destruction of Jerusalem, they opened their discourses with statements of thanks and respect for the local residents who made their homes available to the members of the gathering.

when the person performed the mitzvah.[194] That angel had previously suffered pain, for when the person thought about doing the mitzvah in his home, he created the soul of the angel; whereas, when he performed the mitzvah, he created its body. But because he delayed in creating the body by stopping to talk, the angel also comes to stop him in the middle of the way so that he cannot run and becomes afraid.

This is the meaning of "Righteousness shall go before him." The simple meaning is that all of a person's mitzvos go before him after his death. However, you should make sure that when you go to perform a mitzvah or to pray in synagogue that you do so quickly, and not sluggishly, so that "he will set his steps on the way," — they will not stop you when you cross the river.

Tzava'as HaRivash p. 14a

---

[194] Every mitzvah we do creates an angel.

CHAPTER 15

BO

"And Moses said: 'Thus says the L•rd: At about midnight, I will go out in the midst of Egypt.'"
Bo 11:4

15.1 The main thing is that one's intentions be for the sake of G•d, even when one's deeds are questionable, such as in the case of the Lot's daughters.[195] And if you raise a objection from the case of Baal Pe'or, where the people's intentions were pure, but they were punished anyway,[196] we would have to say that this requires deep contemplation and deliberation, to know whether

---

[195] After the destruction of Sodom and Gomorrah, Lot's daughters engaged their father in an incestuous act; however, their intentions were for the best, as the verses say: "And the first born said unto the younger: 'Our father is old, and there is not a man in the earth to come in unto us after the manner of all the earth. Come, let us make our father drink wine, and we will lie with him, that we may preserve seed of our father.' (*Genesis 19:31,32*).

[196] "And Israel joined himself to Baal Pe'or, and the anger of the L•rd was kindled against Israel" (*Numbers 25:3*). The *Zohar 3:238a* explains that this was done unintentionally. The worship of Baal Pe'or included defecating in front of the idol. The Israelites saw this, and assumed it to be an act of desecration, and so unwittingly participated in the ceremony.

BO

one is acting for the sake of G•d, or not.[197] One should seclude oneself and study Torah to attain a level of objectivity. Then the verse will apply: "And G•d said, Let there be light" (*Genesis 1:3*). That is, G•d will enlighten you from His Torah as to how to proceed. This corresponds to something I wrote elsewhere, on the verse: "At about midnight, I will go out in the midst of Egypt." Doubt occurs at midnight when an issue can go either way.[198] Then "I will go out among Egypt" into a person's limited awareness,[199] to enlighten him.

Ben Poras Yosef, p. 18a

---

[197] Literally, "If it is for G•d or for Azazel" — a reference to the Yom Kippur service (*Leviticus 16*), in which two identical goats were used: one sacrificed in the Temple, and the other sent to a demon in the wilderness. The Baal Shem Tov uses the latter as a metaphor for one's own ego.

[198] I.e., midnight represents the midpoint between the two possibilities.

[199] The Hebrew word for Egypt, "*Mitzrayim*," is related to the word *metzer*, which means narrowness or constriction.

EXODUS

"This month shall be to you . . . "*Bo 12:2* G•d showed Moses the new moon, and said, 'When you see it like this, sanctify.'"[200]

15.2 There is a tradition from the Baal Shem Tov that a person should fast on the eve of each Rosh Chodesh until the *molad*.[201]

Tzror HaChayim, p. 10b

"This month shall be unto you the beginning of months; it shall be the first month of the year to you." *Bo 12:2*

15.3 I heard from my grandfather [the Baal Shem Tov] that once, in the month of Nissan, he told the famous Maggid of Turtshin [the Maggid of Mezritch], "Right now we have to pray, because the first of Nissan is the New Year for Kings,[202] when all

---

[200] *Rosh Hashanah 20a.*
[201] The astronomical moment when the new moon appears. The Baal Shem Tov is expounding on the word "sanctify," in the Sages' statement. That is, on the eve of Rosh Chodesh, you should sanctify yourself by fasting, until the appearance of the new moon.
[202] The Mishna (*Rosh Hashanah 1:1*) lists four New Years of the year: the first of Elul begins the new year for counting animal tithes, the first of Tishrei begins the

the rulers and officials in the world are appointed.[203] At this moment, some rulers who are not good are being appointed, and we must pray [on behalf of Israel].

Degel Machane Ephraim, Bo

"And it came to pass at midnight, that the L•rd smote all the firstborn in the land of Egypt, from the firstborn of Pharaoh that sat on his throne to the firstborn of the captive that was in the dungeon . . ." *Bo 12:29*

15.4 The verse says: "For L•rd G•d (YHVH Elokim) is a sun and a shield" (*Psalms 84:12*). The name YHVH is compared to the sun, [and the name Elokim] to a screen that shields us from its rays. For just as it is impossible to gaze at the light of the sun except through a filter, which allows the weak of vision to benefit from its rays, so the light of

---

counting of Sabbatical and Jubilee years, the first (or the fifteenth) of Shevat begins the tithing cycle for fruit trees, and the first of Nissan is the new year for counting the reign of kings, as well as the yearly festival cycle.

[203] See *Likutey Moharan I:70* and *II:5,10*, where a similar statement is made.

EXODUS

G•d's name YHVH is so intense that it must be diminished and contained within the name Elokim, which has the equivalent numerical value as the word "nature."[204]

Thus, our Sages taught: "In the future, G•d will take the sun out of its shield, the righteous will be healed by it, and the wicked will be judged in it."[205] That is, [He will take the name YHVH] out of the name Elokim — nature — which now conceals it. Then the verse will be fulfilled: "And your eyes shall behold your Master" (*Isaiah 30:20*). G•d will

---

[204] It is impossible for human beings, in their present state of existence, to perceive G•d through His name YHVH, as G•d said to Moses: "No man shall see Me and live" (*Exodus 33:20*). Instead, G•d conceals this revelation within the natural order of creation, corresponding to the name Elokim.

[205] *Nedarim 8b*, on the verses from Malachi: "For, behold, the day comes, it burns like a furnace; and all the proud, and all that work wickedness, shall be stubble; and the day that comes shall set them ablaze, says the L•rd of hosts, and it shall leave them neither root nor branch. But for you who fear My name, the sun of righteousness shall arise with healing in its wings; and you shall go forth, and gambol as calves out of the stall." (*Malachi 3:19,20*) See also, *Isaiah 30:26*: "Moreover the light of the moon shall be as the light of the sun, and the light of the sun shall be sevenfold, as the light of the seven days, in the day that the L•rd binds up the bruise of His people and heals the stroke of their wound."

BO

lead them above the natural order, and they will perceive His great light and compassion. The wicked, however, will be burned by [this revelation], as the prophet said: "YHVH will go forth as a mighty man." (*Isaiah 42:13*) That is, even though the name YHVH represents the attribute of compassion, when it leaves of its "sheath," it wreaks vengeance like a warrior. Because for the wicked, the trait of Compassion is transformed to the trait of Judgment.[206] As the verses say: "And YHVH smote all the firstborn in the land of Egypt,"[207] and "And YHVH said: 'I will blot out man whom I have created from the face of the earth'" (*Genesis 6:7*).

Kesser Shem Tov, part 2, p. 24c

---

[206] In the World to Come, the revelation of G•d will be perceived differently by each individual. Those who lived lives of holiness will have the vessels to perceive this light in a way that heals. Those whose lives are impure will experience this revelation as a destructive force.

[207] See *Exodus 11:4*: "Thus says the L•rd: At about midnight, I will go out in the midst of Egypt," which Unkelos translates as "I will *reveal* myself in the midst of Egypt." In other words, the same revelation which killed the Egyptian firstborn brought about the redemption of the Jews. See R. Tzadok HaKohen of Lublin, *Tzidkas HaTzadik 171*, for a similar idea.

CHAPTER 16

BESHALACH

"And Moses took the bones of Joseph with him." *Beshalach 13:19*

About Moses, the verse says, "The wise of heart take commandments" *Proverbs 10:8* — *Beshalach Rabbah 20:17*

16.1 Why does the verse use the plural, instead of the singular: "The wise of heart takes a commandment"? Because a person must unite the physical act of the commandment, called the "lower mitzvah," with the thought and intention underlying the commandment, which is the "supernal mitzvah." This is also why we say, "Blessed are You . . . who has sanctified us with His commandments" — in the plural.

Ohr Ganuz LaTzaddikim, Vayareh

"And Moses said unto the people: Fear not, stand still, and see the salvation of the L•rd . . . for as you have seen the Egyptians today, you shall see them no more forever." *Beshalach 14:13*

BESHALACH

16.2 That is, by seeing them today, you will cause it that you will never see them again.[208]

Unknown source

"And they believed in G•d, and in Moses His servant." *Beshalach 14:31*

16.3 I heard from my master, the Baal Shem Tov, that "belief" means the mystical attachment of the soul to the Holy One, blessed be He.

Toldot Yaakov Yosef, Ki Tavo

---

[208] The Baal Shem Tov teaches that all creation contains sparks of holiness that must be uplifted and returned to G•d. Sparks can be redeemed by eating kosher food, using an object in a religious context, of even seeing a thing. On this verse, R. Tzadok HaKohen of Lublin (*Tzidkas HaTzadik 105*) explains that each time Moses saw Pharaoh, prior to each of the Ten Plagues, he removed a spark of holiness that was trapped in him. Now, when the entire Jewish nation beheld the Egyptians, they removed all the sparks of holiness that remained in them, without which, the Egyptians could not survive; therefore, nothing remaining of them to see in the future.

EXODUS

"The enemy said: I will pursue, I will overtake, I will divide the spoil; my lust shall be satisfied upon them . . ." *Beshalach 15:9*

16.4 The first five words of this verse begin with the letter *aleph*,[209] because the Master of the World (*Alupho shel Olam*) is hidden there, in the mystery of the name Sa'l.[210] *Toldot Yaakov Yosef, Bereishit, p.8c*

16.5 This applies when the enemy knows that it is doing the will of G•d,[211] but when they only act to fill their own desires — "my lust shall be satisfied upon them" — then they are punished: "You blew

---

h[209] *Omar oyev, erdof, asig, achalek* — אָמַר אוֹיֵב אֶרְדֹף אַשִׂיג אֲחַלֵּק.

[210] סא״ל — one of the 72 names of G•d, that closely resembles the name of the angel Sam'el, סמא״ל, who is appointed over evil. The Talmud states that in the World to Come, G•d will slaughter the evil inclination (*Succah 52a*). According to the Baal Shem Tov, this means that G•d will make the evil inclination "kosher," by removing the bad from it: symbolized, here, by the letter *mem*. Then, only the name סא״ל will remain, which has the combined numerical equivalent of G•d's two names, Y — H — V — H and Ado — nai (91). This is the meaning of the verse: "On that day, G•d (Y — H — V —H) and His name (Ado—nai) will be One" (*Zechariah 14:9*); for the result will be a revelation of G•d's Oneness.

[211] I.e., then G•d's name is with them.

BESHALACH

with Your wind, the sea covered them; they sank like lead in the mighty waters." *Beshalach 15:10.*

Toldot Yaakov Yosef, Ki Tetze, p.102b

16.6 There are five *alephs* in these words, because the Master of the World is hidden there, in order to bring [the Jewish people] close to Him, as the verse says: "And Pharaoh drew near" *Beshalach 14:10.*[212]

Toldot Yaakov Yosef, Genesis, p.34d

"And it was, when Pharaoh let the people go, that G•d did not lead them by way of the land of the Philistines, for it was near; for G•d said: 'Perhaps the people will lose heart when they see war, and return to Egypt.' But G•d led the people indirectly, by the way of the wilderness by the Red Sea . . . . . ." *Beshalach 13:17,18*

---

[212] The word uses the transitive form of the verb "to draw near," *hikriv* (הקריב), which literally means, "he drew others near." According to the Baal Shem Tov, G•d clothes Himself even in the source of affliction, in order to draw us back to Him. See *Pirkei d'Rabbi Eliezer, chapter 42*, on this verse.

EXODUS

16.7 When the masculine [letters] of the Tetragrammaton come first,[213] the forces of Loving — kindness prevail; if not, forgetfulness rules, which is called "Pharaoh."[214] For a human being is a microcosm, and has within him Pharaoh and Egypt. The verse, then, is teaching us the path of repentance; that it should be level after level — "indirectly" — and not all at once. For were that so,

---

[213] The four letters of the Tetragrammaton can be divided into two sets of two: the *yud* — *hey* correspond to the Sefiros of *Chochmah* and *Binah*, and the *vav* — *hey* correspond to *Tiferes* and *Malchus*. *Chochmah* is considered masculine in regards to *Binah*, as is *Tiferes* in relationship to *Malchus*. Kabbalah considers the masculine *Sefiros* to be the source of beneficence, whereas the feminine *Sefiros*, in as much as they create a vessel for containing spiritual downflow, are considered an expression of limitation and Judgment. Furthermore, the four letters of the Name can be arranged in twelve different patterns. When the letters *yud* and *vav* come first, it symbolizes an abundance of Divine compassion; when the letters *hey* come first, it symbolizes an excess of *din* and concealment. The verse from Exodus, cited above, begins "*Vayehi beshalach...*" — וַיְהִי בְּשַׁלַּח. The letters of the first word contain the four letters of the Tetragrammaton, with the letters *vav* and *yud* coming first.

[214] The word "Pharaoh" shares the same letters as the word "*oref*" (neck), and the two concepts correspond. See *Sefer Baal Shem Tov on the Torah, parashas Va'era 5764, footnote 6*.

BESHALACH

a person would be completely annihilated.[215] Thus it is written: "And it was, when Pharaoh let the people go" — these are the limbs of the body that were enslaved to Pharaoh til now. But now, he lets the people — the limbs — go out to freedom. "But G•d did not lead them by way of the land of the Philistines" — for there is a [spiritual] concept called "way." This is the [holy] Names *S'ag* and *Ekiyeh Ka'sa*,[216] which have the numerical value of *derech* ("way").[217] Even the wicked draw sustenance from there, for it is unblemished by human sin, as it says: "If you sinned, what did you do against Him?" *Job 35:6* [218] For this reason, repentance

---

[215] If a person's repentance would bring him too quickly into high levels of perfection, his being would be annihilated. Thus, G•d leads him on the path of repentance slowly, so that his being can grow as a whole.

[216] The Name *S'ag* refers to the Tetragrammaton spelled out as follows: יו״ד ד״י וא״ו ד״י which has the numerical value of 63 (ס״ג). (The letter *hey* in the Name is written here with a *dalet*, so as not to unnecessarily write the Holy Name.) This corresponds to the world of *Binah*. Likewise, the name *Ekiyeh*, when spelled out as follows, corresponds to *Binah*: אל״ף ה״י יו״ד ה״י. It has the numerical value of 161 (קס״א).

[217] The word *derech* (דרך) has the numerical value of 224, equal to the two Divine Names.

[218] The wicked draw benefit from this spiritual world because it is a source of pure beneficence. However,

helps, for the damage of sin does not reach there. [For instance,] a person who commits adultery arouses in the [upper] world the aspect of love.[219] Only in the world below do his sins have a bad effect. But when he repents, his deeds have a positive effect, and he repairs everything, for he uplifts the [lower] levels to Binah, which is *Ekiyeh.*

Thus, the verse says: "G•d did not lead them by way of the land of the Philistines." For from this "way,"[220] the Land of the Philistine, the impure shells, also derive nourishment. G•d did not lead them that way, "for it was near" — that is, it was near to forgetfulness, which is called Pharaoh, lest they see this aspect, which is called "way," as we explained above . . . . . For as soon as they realize this, they come close to returning to Pharaoh, who

---

they do not receive this sustenance directly, but rather "behind the back," as one would give to one's enemy, indirectly. (See *Sefer HaTanya, chap. 6*). The Baal Shem Tov will explain below that were evil to receive a direct illumination from this world, it would become empowered more.

[219] As we have discussed elsewhere, immoral lusts are a fallen form of the pure love of G•d. The higher one rises on the ladder of the worlds, the more the pure essence of any act is revealed, while the outward, impure manifestation falls away.

[220] I.e., the way of direct repentance.

BESHALACH

is forgetfulness. Therefore, "G•d led the people indirectly . . . . ."[221]

Kesser Shem Tov 110 [222]

"Then G•d said to Moses: 'Behold, I will make bread rain down to you from heaven; and the people will go out and gather enough for each day . . . . ." *Beshalach 16:4*

16.8 A poor person has the privilege of speaking to the Holy One every day. A rich person, however, receives all his sustenance from G•d at once, and doesn't need to ask Him for his daily requirements — not unless he is very righteous, and realizes that everything he owns is worthless, without G•d giving it life force to sustain him. The proof is that a sick person has all the food he needs, but still cannot sustain himself.

---

[221] The Baal Shem Tov seems to be saying that if G•d were to lead a person along a direct path of repentance, which means the revelation that at the root of all his sins — in the World of *Binah* — everything is in fact good, then the evil inclination— the Philistines, who also derive sustenance from that world — would be empowered, and cause a person to return again to Pharaoh — Forgetfulness.

[222] See also *Toldot Yaakov Yosef, p. 53b.*

EXODUS

A poor person, with nothing to eat, must beseech G•d each day. Thus, he merits speaking to Him every day. Furthermore, G•d must also remember the poor person daily, to arrange his livelihood. However, G•d does not need to remember a rich person each day, for He already gave him everything at one time.

Rav Yebi, Tehilim

CHAPTER 17

YISRO

"And Moses brought forth the people out of the camp to meet G•d; and they stood at the bottom of the mountain." *Yisro 19:17*

17.1 Our Sages said that G•d uprooted Mount Sinai and held it over the Israelites' heads like a barrel, "If you accept My Torah, good," He said. "If not, this will be your grave."[223] This teaches that even when you do not feel like studying Torah and serving G•d, "you are not free to desist from it."[224] Imagine that someone is forcing you. This is a good approach for periods of small — mindedness.[225] You should never stop studying or serving G•d, even when you

---

[223] *Shabbat 88a.*
[224] *Pirkei Avos 2:3.*
[225] Literally, "Days of Smallness." Smallness and Largeness (Katnus and Gadlut) are kabbalistic terms describing various stages in the development of the Sefiros. Lower Sefiros move from Smallness to Largeness when the higher Sefiros, corresponding to the intellectual faculties, enter into them. The Baal Shem Tov applies these terms to the human psyche, which at times can perceive something of G•d's light and feel a purpose to existence, while at other times, loses the vision and falls into constricted consciousness. See Sefer Baal Shem Tov, parashas Vayerah, for more on this idea.

YISRO

lack the desire, for at least you are performing the action.[226]

Ben Poras Yosef, Vayeshev, p. 66d

"And G•d spoke all these words, saying, 'I am the L•rd Your G•d.'" *Yisro 20:1,2*

17.2 The Talmud says that the word "I" — *Anochi* — is an acronym for the words, "I gave over My soul in writing."[227] For the Torah corresponds to the human being, as the verse says: "This is the Torah — man" (*Numbers 19:14*).[228] Just as a human being has 258 limbs and 365 sinews, so the Torah has 248 positive commandments and 365 negative commandments.[229] Each commandment

---

[226] The Baal Shem Tov taught that the main reward we receive for observing Torah and mitzvos comes from the efforts ma de during the times of Smallness. See *Ben Poras Yosef, parashas Vayeshev*.

[227] Ana nafshai ketavit yehavit. אנא נפשאי כתבית יהבית. (Shabbat 105a.)

[228] The verse should read: "This is the Torah (the Law) of a man who dies in his tent..." However, in Hebrew, the preposition "of" is missing, so that the verse can be interpreted as the Baal Shem Tov does here.

[229] The Sages of the Talmud describe the human body as being composed of this many limbs and sinews, though their exact anatomical division is unknown to us. See

EXODUS

corresponds to a particular organ, giving it life from the source of that commandment. Thus, a person's life flows from the entire Torah. And just as there are five aspects of the soul: the *nefesh, ruach, neshama, chaya* and *yechidah*, so the holy Torah has a body [230] and a soul, which is its hidden dimension. [Together they comprise] *PaRDeS*.[231] Thus the word *Anochi* means "I gave over My soul in writing" — "My soul" refers to the Torah.[232]

Degel Machane Ephraim, Ha'Azinu

17.3 I heard in the name of my Master (the Baal Shem Tov) that just as the Ten Commandments contain the entire Torah, as Rav Sa'adiah Gaon

---

Makos 23b; *Zohar 1:170b*, on the correspondence to the commandments.

[230] This refers to the revealed aspects of the Torah: the Written and Oral Torah, and the Legal Codes.

[231] Literally, "an orchard," but used as an acronym for the four modes of Torah interpretation: Peshat — literal, Remez — symbolic, Derush — homiletic, and Sod — mystical.

[232] The Baal Shem Tov is implying that the very essence of G•d is hidden within the holy Torah, as the Zohar says: "The Torah and the Holy One are one" (*Zohar 3:73a*).

YISRO

wrote, so the whole Torah is included in every single one of its words.[233]

Ben Poras Yosef, p.23d

"Remember the Sabbath day, to keep it holy."
Yisro 20:8

17.4 On the eve of Shabbos, during the Mincha and Kabbalas Shabbos prayers, a person raises up all the words and mitzvos of the previous week, because that is the time when the worlds ascend.

Tzivos HaRivash, part 2, p. 4b

17.5 Once, when the Baal Shem Tov recited the Kabbalas Shabbos prayers in the field, all the flocks

---

[233] On a simple level, this is because each Hebrew letter contains within it all the 22 letters of the alphabet, of which the Torah is comprised. For example, a letter can be divided into component parts to derive other letters (the letter aleph, א, can be divided into a vav with two yuds, 'ו'); alternatively, each letter can be spelled out in full (aleph = aleph, lamed, phey), and then again, until the entire alphabet is obtained. On a deeper level, the Baal Shem Tov is alluding to the absolute unity of the Torah, in which, like a hologram, even the smallest unit contains within it all the rest.

gathered around him and bleated the entire time he was praying.

It is said that with his prayers, he lifted up all of the lower levels, until even the flocks and the herds attained a realization of G•d, and cried out with him.[234]

Divrei Elimelech, Bechukosai

"And all the people saw the voices, and the fire and the voice of the shofar, and the mountain smoking." *Yisro 20:14*

17.6 When the Baal Shem Tov would teach Torah to his holy students, they would be surrounded by fire. The ministering angels would gather around them, and they could hear the thunder and lightning, and the words "I am the L•rd your G•d," from the mouth of G•d Himself.

This is well known to all.

Heichal HaBracha, Va'Eschanan, p. 28a

---

[234] See Toldot Adam, p. 58, who says this happened when the Baal Shem Tov recited the words: "He lifted up the destitute from poverty, and makes his families like a flock" (Psalms 107:41).

"And Jethro, Moses' father — in — law, took a burnt offering and sacrifices for G•d; and Aaron and all the elders of Israel came to eat bread with Moses' father — in — law before G•d." *Yisro 8:12*

17.7 Nowhere in the Torah do we find it saying that Moses ate. In fact, we find only the opposite: "And he was there with G•d forty days and nights; he did not eat bread, nor drink water" (*Exodus 34:28*). We also find: "And Aaron and all the elders of Israel came to eat bread with Moses' father — in — law before G•d."[235]

This is because Moses' eating was so spiritual that is impossible to write in the Torah that it was in this world. It was not a physical eating at all, but extremely spiritual.

Zera Kodesh, rimzei Pesach

"And on the next day, Moses sat to judge the people; and the people stood around Moses from morning to evening." *Yisro 18:13*

---

[235] Moses was surely there, but is not mentioned in the verse.

EXODUS

Any judge who judges with absolute truth, even one hour a day, is considered by the Torah as though he were G•d 's partner in the work of creation.[236]

". . . . . with absolute truth" — as opposed to a deceitful judgment.[237]

17.8 I heard from my Master (the Baal Shem Tov) an explanation of the Gemara's admonition to judge truthfully. The two attributes of *Chesed* and *Gevurah* borrow from each other and are included in each another. When they join together, they make *Tiferes*. This happens through the judges, who are the "three heads." Therefore, they must hate illicit gain[238] — *"Botza"* — which is formed

---

[236] Shabbat 10a, quoted in Rashi on this verse.
[237] Tosefos, Shabbat 10a, s.v. din emes l'amiso. A deceitful judgment is based upon the false testimony of the witnesses. That is, if a judge knows that the witnesses are lying, but cannot prove it, he is still not obligated to closely analyze their words. This is judging with absolute truth. To heed the false words of the witnesses would be to issue a deceitful judgment. (See Tosefos, Bava Basra 8b, s.v. din emes l'amiso.)
[238] As the verse says: "Now, you (Moshe) should seek out from among all the people capable, God — fearing men — men of truth, who hate unjust gain, and appoint them over [the people] as leaders of thousands, leaders of hundreds, leaders of fifties, and leaders of tens. And

YISRO

from the second letters of the names A**b**raham, Yitzchak, Ya**a**kov.[239] When they clarify [the dispute] and are united in their thinking, they attain "absolute truth." Furthermore, below, there exists gold and silver dross that steal from each other.[240] Through the judges, these traits are refined.

Toldot Yaakov Yosef, p. 209a

---

let them judge the people at all times" (Exodus 18:21,22).

[239] Abraham, Isaac and Jacob (Avraham, Yitzchak and Yaakov) also correspond to Chesed, Gevurah and Tiferes. The second letters of their names, however, represent the forces of concealment. Thus, they spell out botza — illicit gain.

[240] Due to the primordial "breaking of the vessels," each of the supernal attributes also has a fallen manifestation. For instance, love of G•d falls to the level of material lusts, awe of G•d falls to the level of mortal fears. These fallen emotions must be refined of their "dross" and uplifted to the service of G•d. Silver and gold correspond to the Sefiros of Chesed, Gevurah. Rather than combining together positively to serve, as do the supernal qualities, they "steal" from one another. (Only when the various attributes of the personality are used in the service of G•d can opposite combine, as in the verse: "rejoice with trembling" (Psalms 2:11).) In the act of judging truthfully, the judges purify the fallen attributes and uplift them to their source in holiness.

EXODUS

"And you shall teach them the statutes and the laws, and shall show them the way which they should go, and the work that they must do."
Yisro 18:20

17.9 By way of example, deep in a forest is a den of robbers who constantly send out men to entice and lead people to them, so that they can kill them and steal their money. A wise person, however, will refuse to go. This is the meaning of "the way which they should go." That is, the straight way, and not after the enticements of the evil inclination that seeks to destroy them.

Degel Machane Ephraim, Vayeshev

CHAPTER 18

MISHPATIM

"These are the ordinances that you shall set before them." *Mishpatim 21:1*

18.1 On this verse, the Zohar says: "These are the cycles of reincarnation . . . . ."[241] This is a surprising connection, seeing that the subsequent verses speak about monetary laws. However, I heard the following explanation: One person accuses another in court [that he owes him money]. Though the defendant knows he is innocent, the Torah nevertheless obligates him to pay. He shouldn't be plagued by the question, "isn't it a Torah of truth, whose 'paths are pleasant?'" because this *is* the truth of the Torah and its pleasantness. How can this be so? Undoubtedly, he owed this money to the other man in a previous incarnation, and the Torah is now making him pay in order to free him from this debt. As for the person who took the money deceitfully, he will have to give his own accounting in the future. This is only one example of many possible cases.

This is what the holy Zohar alludes to in its reading of the verse: "These are the ordinances." For while the law may at times seem unjust, really, "these are the cycles of reincarnation." The Creator

---

[241] *Zohar 2:94a.*

of the world and of all souls knows what occurred between individuals in previous lives, and directs His world according to the Torah, with love and compassion, with righteousness and true justice.

The implications of this are very broad.

Degel Machane Ephraim, Mishpatim

"Do not put your hand with the wicked to be an unrighteous witness." *Mishpatim 23:1*

18.2 You must never say anything bad about any Jew, G•d forbid, because then you will have to serve as an "unrighteous witness." When the evil inclination accuses someone, he will call you to bear witness to his words.[242]

If you must speak disparagingly about some bad trait or person, you should state clearly that you are not referring to any specific individual, but

---

[242] R. Moshe of Peshavorsk explained that when the evil inclination rises above to indict a Jew, his words are not heeded, since he is only one voice, and the Torah says: "According to two witnesses . . . shall the matter be established" (*Deuteronomy 19:15*). Thus, he waits until another individual also speaks badly about the person. Then, he joins with him, to bear witness and accuse (*Hakdamos Likutey Torah v'Shas*).

MiSHPATIM

only to the bad character trait itself. *Rishpei Aish, Mishpatim 44*

18.3 One Rosh Hashana, when the disciples of the Baal Shem Tov were praying together, one of them dropped a snuff box, and bent down in the middle of his prayers to retrieve it. Another of the disciples saw this, and severely berated him for interrupting his prayers just to take a whiff of tobacco. The Baal Shem Tov, with his spiritual insight, realized that the rebuke of his holy disciple had brought a heavenly judgment upon his friend, to die within the coming year. The Baal Shem Tov made a "soul ascension," and argued fiercely before the Heavenly Court, to no avail. He continued trying, and on the night of Hoshana Rabbah,[243] his soul ascended one last time, and he argued and cried out in prayer. Finally, it was agreed that if the accuser himself would judge his friend favorably, the latter would be delivered from the verdict.

The Baal Shem Tov entered the study hall and found the disciple who had chastised his friend

---

[243] According to Kabbalah, the verdict issued on Rosh Hashana, and considered during the entire holiday period, is finally handed over to the Heavenly Court on the night of Hoshana Rabbah (the last night of Succot). From then on, it can no longer be rescinded.

reciting the book of Deuteronomy.244 The Baal Shem Tov took away his ability to concentrate,245 making it impossible for him to recite the verses with the appropriate attachment to G•d. The student began to pace the study hall, contemplating on the greatness of G•d, His Oneness, and other matters (in order to regain his concentration). Suddenly, a thought entered his mind. "Why is it that the tobacco plant has only recently been discovered, making it possible now for people to snuff or smoke it?246 Perhaps there are souls in our generations too sublime to be clothed in the physical world, and that the only way to rectify them is through something equally refined, like the sense of smell." This led him to feelings of regret over the anger he had showed his friend; for

---

244 There is a custom to recite the entire book of Deuteronomy on the night of Succot, as the following days are Shemini Atzerus and Simchos Torah, when the yearly cycle of Torah reading is complete.
245 Literally, "he took away his 'mind' (*mochin*)," which refers, as well, to higher states of consciousness.
246 Tobacco was introduced into Eastern Europe in about 1600, one hundred years before the birth of the Baal Shem Tov.

MiSHPATIM

who knows which souls he raised up by snuffing tobacco with the mystical intentions?

On the day of Hoshana Rabbah, it was the Baal Shem Tov's custom to answer all questions about what had been decreed above and below, and about what would happen throughout the world (in the coming year), for with his divinely inspired knowledge, he could see from one end of the earth to the other. On that day, he was in especially good spirits. Each of his students prepared a different question, some in areas of Torah discourse, and some with questions on the Talmud, or other matters. The Baal Shem Tov would answer them all.

That disciple, who had berated his friend, chose to ask his question about the discovery of tobacco. When he presented his question, the Baal Shem Tov said to him, "Tell me what you think!" He gave his reason, and the Baal Shem Tov said, "But say more! Tell me all the thoughts that you had last night." The student remembered what he had thought, and told the Baal Shem Tov how he had judged his friend favorably. At that moment, the heavenly decree was annulled. The Baal Shem Tov was then able to tell him the whole story, about what he had brought upon his friend. And he warned him always to judge G•d fearing people favorably, so as not to bring supernal judgments upon them, that it should always be good for them.

Otzar HaChaim, Kedoshim, p. 171c

"And you shall serve the L•rd your G•d, and He will bless your bread, and your water." *Mishpatim 23:25*

18.4 When you speak words of Torah during your meals, the words become the soul for the physicality [of the food] that is on the table. You should always speak a lot of Torah over your meals — during the week, and all the more so, on Shabbos.

Kesser Shem Tov, part 2, p. 4b

CHAPTER 19

TERUMAH

EXODUS

"And the L•rd spoke to Moses, saying: Speak to the children of Israel, that they take for Me an offering; of every man whose heart prompts him, you shall take My offering."

Terumah 25:1,2

19.1 A person should seek ways to transform his mundane desires[247] — all that "his heart prompts him" — into good qualities. And from his habitual, bad traits, he should learn how to serve the Creator with the same passion and desire, even more intensely.

Tiferes Shlomo, Toldot

19.2 I heard from my Master [the Baal Shem Tov], in the name of Rabbi Sa'adiah Gaon, that it is appropriate to desire all kinds of material things, and through this, to come to a desire for Torah and serving G•d.

Ben Poras Yosef, Vayechi, p. 85b

19.3 I heard a parable from my Master. A king had a son whom he wanted to teach the various

---

[247] Literally, "external desires" (*tava'ot chitzonim*). See below, where the Baal Shem Tov explains that within every mundane desire the love of G•d can be found.

TERUMAH

subjects that were required for a prince to know. He hired several scholars, but the boy failed to grasp even a single area of knowledge, The king finally gave up on him, and only one sage remained. One day, the king's son saw a beautiful, young woman,[248] and desired her. The sage complained about this to the king, but the king replied that since the boy shows some desire, even a physical one, it is possible for him to learn all the fields of knowledge. The king ordered that the young woman be brought to the palace, and told her that should she must not listen to the prince's solicitations, unless he agrees to master one branch of knowledge. Afterwards, she should demand that he learn yet another branch. This continued until he mastered all the areas of study. But when he finally became a wise man, he rejected the young woman and married a princess, as was fitting for him.[249]

The meaning of the parable is obvious.

Ben Poras Yosef, Vayechi, p. 88a

---

[248] According to another version of this parable, the girl was a harlot.
[249] The other version concludes, "for what connection should a prince have with a harlot."

EXODUS

How fair and how pleasant are you, lover of delights. *Song of Songs 7:7*

19.4 How fair and how pleasant it is that in all [mundane] delights there is the Supernal Love. Because when one's innate desires are evoked, it becomes easier to love G•d. Otherwise, it is difficult to develop these emotions, and to start to love Him. Understand this!

Furthermore, whenever a person feels a spontaneous attraction toward a certain pleasure, which is a love that has "fallen" from its supernal source, he should realize that G•d is helping him, and making it easier to love Him. G•d knows that the person would otherwise never feel this emotion. But if the person fails to realize this, and is drawn after that pleasure itself, he casts down the [Supernal Love] even further.

At other times, a person may have a negative desire, G•d forbid, such as to commit a sin, yet some obstacle prevents him from doing it. G•d is helping him here, as well. For when G•d sees that the person lacks the consciousness to uplift the fallen love to its source — to the love of G•d — and chooses instead to follow evil, G•d then "contracts" Himself even more, to place before him an obstacle.[250] At least then, the person will remain passive and avoid damaging himself further.

Me'or Einayim, Va'Eschanan

---

[250] G•d clothes Himself in physical desires in order to allow people the opportunity to transcend them, and transform them into a desire for Him. However, if the person cannot find G•d there, and comes close to sinning, G•d lowers Himself even more, to clothe Himself in the very force which now prevents him from carrying out the act.

CHAPTER 20

TETZAVAH

"And Aaron shall bear the names of the children of Israel on the Breastplate of Judgment upon his heart, when he goes into the holy place, for a memorial before the L•rd continually. And you shall put in the Breastplate of Judgment the Urim and the Thummim; and they shall be upon Aaron's heart, when he goes in before the L•rd . . . . . " *Tetzahah 28:29,30*

20.1 It is known that the Breastplate barely contained all twenty—two letters of the Hebrew alphabet, as our Sages have said.[251] Therefore, when they had to ask a question[252] that used several of the same letters, such as "Should I go to

---

[251] *Yoma* 73b. There were twelve precious stones set in the Breastplate of Judgment. They were engraved with the names of the Patriarchs, Abraham, Isaac and Jacob, the names of the twelve tribes, and the words "tribes of Yeshurun." Certain letters, such as the *gimel* or the *zayin,* were written only once.

[252] The Breastplate of Judgment was a prophetic device, worn by the High Priest, through which questions could be asked of G•d. When the king or the High Court (Sanhedrin) would ask a question, the Priest would see various letters sparkle or bulge out. Using Divine Inspiration, he would then be able to combine the letters to spell out the answer. See Aryeh Kaplan, *Handbook of Jewish Thought*, vol. 1 (New York: Moznaim, 1979), 6:36 and fn. 110, for more on this subject.

TETZAVAH

Bavel,"[253] how were they answered? There is a very great mystery in this . . . I heard from my grandfather [the Baal Shem Tov], that each of the twenty two letters [of the Hebrew alphabet] contains within it all the other letters of the alphabet[254] (except for the letter *mem*[255]). Since G•d commanded that all twenty—two letters be inscribed on the Breastplate, when the priest would be enwrapped in Divine inspiration, the letters would shine in their expanded forms. This enabled them to receive everything they needed to know. Understand this!

---

[253] The question "Should I go to Bavel?" contains two letters *beit*, and three *lameds* —האלך לבבל. However, it is likely that the author was only using this as an example of a phrase with repeating letters, because there were at least five *beits* and four *lameds* in the Breastplate — enough to spell out these words.

[254] These can be attained by spelling out each letter in full. For instance, writing out the letter *aleph* in full provides a *lamed* and a *phey* (אלף). Furthermore, each of these letters can further expanded, to produce even more letters, until the entire Hebrew alphabet is reconstituted.

[255] The letter *mem*, when written in full, will not produce any additional letters — מם. (Original editor's note.)

EXODUS

This is the meaning of "onyx stones, and stones to be set,[256] for the ephod, and for the breastplate" (*Exodus 25:7*).

Degel Machane Ephraim, Likutim

---

[256] "*Avnei miluyim*," read alternatively as "stones that are filled out" — meaning that the engraved letters shone in their expanded forms.

In a number of other lessons on this theme, the Baal Shem Tov explains that additional letters can be derived from a single letter by using the techniques of *gematria* (numerical value of the letters), or by dividing the letters into their component parts. It is possible that those approaches were originally mentioned with this lesson, since there are a number of other letters, such as the *gimel, zayin, ches, tes* and *samech* that could never be derived from the other letters, no matter how many times they are spelled out. See Baal Shem Tov on the Torah, *parashas Yisro*, fn. 11, for more on this subject.

CHAPTER 21

KI TETZAH

EXODUS

"This they shall give, every one that passes among them that are numbered, half a shekel after the shekel of the sanctuary." *Ki Tetzah 30:13*

G•d showed Moses a shekel of fire, and said, "They should give like this."[257]

21.1 A goldsmith had an apprentice. When he finished teaching him the craft, he wrote down for his student all the steps in the process. However, he did not write down that he had to ignite the coals before he started, because that was the main thing, and unnecessary to mention. However, the student forgot, etc.[258]

This parable is easily understood. The main thing [in serving G•d] is that there be a spark of fire that can be ignited.[259]

Ben Poras Yosef, p. 119b

---

[257] *Midrash Tanchuma, Ki Sisa* 9. Quoted by Rashi on the verse.

[258] The parable ends here. Obviously, the student forgot to light the coals, and was unable to produce any results.

[259] The Baal Shem Tov said about the Maggid of Mezritch, when the latter first came to see him, "A box full of candles has come to me. They only need to be lit." (*Zicharon Tov, p.5c*)

KI TETZAH

"And now, if You will forgive their sin; and if not, erase me, please, from Your book which You have written." *Ki Tetzah 32:32*

21.2 How is this an example of Moses' humility, i.e., that his death should be an atonement for the great sin [of the Golden Calf]?

Rather, we must understand the nature of Moses' humility. It is easy to understand the humility of other people which is the insignificance a person feels when compared to others. However, Moses knew the spiritual root and worth of each Jewish soul, as well as the greatness of his own soul, that included within it all the souls of Israel, as the Sages said: "One woman in Egypt gave birth to 600,000 at one time — this is Moses, our Teacher."[260] How, then, could he possibly be humble?

It is written: "All Israel are responsible for one another"[261] — meaning, they are commingled with

---

[260] *Zohar I:25a.*
[261] *Shavuos 39a; Sanhedrin 27b.* The Talmud means that each Jew is responsible for the sins of his fellow, when he is able to prevent them.

one another,[262] for they all share a single root. Therefore, whenever a positive spirit from the source of goodness and holiness[263] enters the world, it affects each and every Jew, according to his or her level. A Tzaddik will be greatly inspired to serve G•d, with great holiness and longing. A person who is not such a Tzaddik will also be inspired, but to a lesser degree. Even a completely wicked person will be moved to thoughts of repentance, albeit only temporarily. Still, he is inspired a little, which may lead him to complete repentance.

The opposite is also true. When a spirit emanates from the side of evil, it also affects each person. The wicked will fall severely and commit a sin; whereas the Tzaddik will experience some [improper] thought, albeit momentarily.

Now, when we see that a wicked person has actually committed a sin, we have to ask, who is to blame? Perhaps the Tzaddik is to blame, because

---

[262] The word for "responsible" — *arev* (literally "guarantor") and the word "mixed together" — *me'orav* share the same root.

[263] Literally, "from the good inclination" — the *yetzer tov*. This does not refer to the individual's good inclination, rather to the source of goodness that radiates into every soul.

the improper thought also came to him, and had he immediately worked to nullify it at its root, the wicked person would not have sinned. On the other hand, perhaps the wicked person is to blame, because once he actually committed the sin, as soon as the thought entered his mind, the Tzaddik could no longer annul it.

This is the essence of Moses' humility. Whenever he saw some bad trait in a Jew, he would blame himself, thinking that it was most likely his fault. This was his intention, when he said, "Erase me, please." That is, "I am the guilty one, not them!" But G•d answered him, "Whoever has sinned against Me, him will I erase from My book." Meaning to say, "I know who is to blame!"

Divrei Moshe, Shemini

21.3 There are two aspects of sin. The first is when the leader of the generation has a sinful thought, which causes the general populace to sin, G•d forbid. The second is when the people sin, which can at times, cause the leader of the generation to have sinful thoughts.

The difference between them is that in the first case, the leader cannot pray on behalf of the people, since the evil started with him. In the second case, the leader was compelled [by the people], and his prayers are still efficacious.

This is what Moses said: "And now, if You will forgive their sin" — that is, if You forgive them [on account of his prayers], then I will know that it is *their* sin, that they committed themselves. "And if not" — if You do not forgive them and my prayers are not accepted, then it is possible that my own thoughts are the cause. Therefore, "erase me, please." Thus, the verse continues: "And the L•rd said to Moses: 'Whoever has sinned against Me, him will I erase from My book."

Imrei Tzaddikim in the name of the *Kedushas Levi*

CHAPTER 22

VAYAKHEL

EXODUS

"Do not burn a fire in any of your dwellings on Shabbat." *Vayakhel 35:3*

22.1 One may move a new lamp [on Shabbat],[264] but not an old one.[265] Rabbi Shimon says, One may move any lamp, except a lamp which burns on Shabbat.[266]

Shabbat 44a

22.2 The human soul is called "a lamp," as it says: "The soul of man is the lamp of G•d" (*Proverbs 20:27*), and the Sages said: "Your lamp is in My hands."[267] According to the holy Zohar, all souls are taken out of Hell on Shabbat, except for those who desecrated Shabbat [during their lives]."[268]

---

[264] The Mishnah discusses the laws of *muktza*, things which are forbidden to move on Shabbat by rabbinic decree. A new oil lamp may be moved if used to hold a permissible substance.

[265] An oil lamp that has already been used cannot be moved on Shabbat, even if it is empty, since it is no longer fit for anything but lighting. (Earthenware lamps of ancient times generally became unsuitable for other purposes after their first use.)

[266] R. Shimon disagrees and states that only lamps that are actually burning on the Shabbat cannot be moved, lest the fire go out.

[267] *Midrash Rabbah, Emor* 31:4.

[268] *Zohar 2:150b.*

VAYAKHEL

This explains the Mishnah above. "One may move a new lamp" — a soul, which is called a lamp, that did not [completely] befoul itself with sin[269] can be moved out of hell on Shabbat; however, an old lamp — a soul that had been entrenched in sin — may not. But R. Shimon says,[270] One may move any lamp except the lamp which burns on Shabbat. A person who desecrated Shabbat will burn in Hell even on the Shabbat, as retribution.

Kesser Shem Tov, part 2, p. 17a

"And Betzalel made the ark . . . . ." *Vayakhel 37:1*

22.3 For the shadow of the Holy One was there, between the Cherubim.[271]

Midrash Tanchuma, VaYakhel 7

---

[269] I.e., which is still relatively new.
[270] R. Shimon's opinion in the Mishna is in keeping with the statement of the Zohar, which he authored.
[271] G•d's "shadow" refers to the Divine Presence that was manifest over the Ark of the Covenant. The name Betzalel means, "In the shadow of G•d." Thus, Betzalel knew how to build the Ark, so that it would be a fitting place for the revelation of G•d.

EXODUS

22.4 The Baal Shem Tov once taught his students the following lesson. Pointing to a cask of beer that was in the room, he said, "This cask is made from clay and formed by human hands. Its material substance is simple, for the main thing is its form, as it is said, 'The last in deed is the first in thought.'[272] Thus, the vessel is actually formed from the craftsman's thoughts, so that the life force of the craftsman is embodied in the life force of the vessel, and his intellect radiates into it. It is therefore possible to discern in the vessel the entire personality and conduct of its maker, just as a branch bears the life force of the root.

"It turns out, then, that I can see in this cask that it was made by a craftsman who had no legs. Now, if the existence of the cask depends upon the presence of his wisdom, were we to remove his wisdom from it, it would lack any unifying factor."

After the class, one of the students lifted the cask and set it on one of the benches. As soon as he did so, the entire cask crumbled into dust, as though it never existed.[273]   *Kisvei Kodesh, p. 26a*

---

[272] From the *Lecha Dodi* prayer recited at the onset of Shabbat. This means that the original intention (of G•d or of an artisan) is reflected in the final product.
[273] Apparently, the Baal Shem Tov removed the life—force from the cask, as he said. See *Ohr HaMeir*, by R.

VAYAKHEL

Zev Wolf of Zhitomer, *parashas Ha'Azinu*, who writes: Once, the Baal Shem Tov heard a wicked man playing on the violin, and could hear in the music all the sins that the man had ever committed. And had he heard the man singing, he could have discerned even more, such as the outcome of all of his sins, because a person puts all of his energy into his singing (therefore revealing more of his soul).

The meaning of the verse from Exodus, quoted above, is that because Betzalel put all of himself into the work of building the Ark, it became an appropriate place for the dwelling of the Divine Presence, itself called the "Shadow of G•d."

CHAPTER 23

PEKUDEI

EXODUS

"These are the accounts of the Tabernacle, the Tabernacle of the Testimony. . ." *Pekudei 38:21*

23.1 We need to understand why, when the parasha list all the details that went into [the construction of] the Tabernacle and the vessels, it concludes each case by stating that it was done "as G•d commanded Moses." Why does it mention this each time, rather than making a general conclusion at the end, that everything was done "as G•d commanded Moses"?

The Torah is teaching a fundamental lesson in the service of G•d and the fulfillment of the commandments, be it shofar, succah, Pesach, tefillin, etc. Each one consists of action, words and intention, i.e., thought. The underlying intentions of the commandments and prayers are great and awesome, and few people, even those on a high spiritual level, grasp more than a minute portion of the intentions that the Men of the Great Assembly put into the prayers.[274] The same holds true in the performance of the commandments.

---

[274] The Men of the Great Assembly (c. 4th century B.C.E.), formalized the prayer service that has been used until today.

PEKUDEI

And yet, every Jew must partake of these three aspects. Because the physical act of the commandment creates a garment for the soul in the lower Gan Eden,[275] and the intention put in the commandment creates a garment for the soul in the higher Gan Eden.

The answer, then, is to include oneself and ones intentions — be it in prayer or in the performance of commandments, in one's weekday meals, and all the more so, in the three meals of Shabbat — with the "perfectly faithful of Israel,"[276] who know the inner meaning of the prayers and the

---

[275] Gan Eden literally means "the Garden of Eden," but refers here to the spiritual dimension that the soul ascends to after death. According to Kabbalah, when the soul leaves the physical body, it enters a spiritual body, called the "Garment of the Rabbis," that is formed of all the good deeds and mitzvos that the individual performed during life. And just as a living person has a physical and a spiritual side, an outer and inner dimension, so the soul after death has an outer dimension, the "Garment of the Rabbis," and an inner dimension, that was formed by the intention one put into the performance of the mitzvos in this world. Furthermore, as the soul continues to ascend after death, the inner dimensions become externalized to become outer garments, and new inner dimensions become revealed. See R. Tzadok HaKohen of Lublin, *Tzidkas HaTzaddik* 155.

[276] I.e. The Tzaddikim.

commandments, according to the Men of the Great Assembly. This is the meaning of the Arizal's statement that one should precede each prayer with the words: "I hereby accept upon myself the positive commandment to shall love your fellow as yourself,'" for then one includes one's own prayers with those who know how to unite the supernal attributes. Let these words be sufficient.

Now, in building the Tabernacle [in the desert], their thoughts were focused on building the Supernal Tabernacle, as the verse says: "And the Tabernacle was erected" (*Exodus 40:17*) — that is, when the Tabernacle below was erected, so was the Tabernacle above.[277] And while their thoughts and intentions were carried out in the physical world below, they had in mind the spiritual world, to build the Tabernacle above, which is the secret of the creation of heaven and earth and all the worlds. However, not every mind can grasp this. Therefore, after the construction of each vessel of the Tabernacle, the people clearly stated that they were doing it according to the inner intention that G•d commanded Moses.

---

[277] *Midrash Tanchuma, Ki Sisa 18; Zohar 2:240a.*

PEKUDEI

This is also as we say [before the performance of each mitzvah]: "May the pleasantness of the L•rd our G•d be upon us, and establish the work of our hands, and establish the work of our hands" (*Psalms 90:17*).

Ben Poras Yosef, Introduction, *p.8, 9*

Appendix

GLOSSARY

Achiyah HaShiloni — The Heavenly teacher of the Baal Shem Tov. In prior incarnations, Achiyah HaShaloni witnessed the exodus from Egypt, was a prophet during the time of King David, and taught Elijah the Prophet.

Amidah — (lit. standing as it is a prayer that is to be recited inaudible in a standing position); also referred to as the Shemonah Esreh (eighteen benedictions); the main section of daily prayer, recited standing and inaudibly.(lit. standing); The main section of daily prayer, recited standing and inaudibly.

Arizal — acronym for Eloki Rabbi Yitzchak — the Divinely inspired Rabbi Yitzcahk Luria (1535 — 1572) — whose teachings became central for virtually all Kabbalistic thought thereafter.

Asiyah — (lit. deed); The final level in the Divine creative process which includes the physical universe.

Atzilus — (lit. emanation); The realm of spiritual existence which, although encompassing attributes which have a specific definition, is in a state of infinity and at one with the Infinite Divine Light.

Beriyah — (lit. creation); The realm of spiritual existence which represents the first beginnings of a consciousness of self.

Binah — (lit. comprehension); The stage of the intellectual process that develops abstract conception, giving it breadth and depth.

Barchu — (lit. bless); One of the responsive readings in congregational prayer.

Chassid — (lit. pious one); One who observes beyond the letter of the law; A follower of the Chassidic movement (pl. Chassidim).

Chazan — (lit. cantor); One who leads the congregation in prayer.

Cheder — (lit. room); A Torah school for young children.

Chesed — (lit. kindness); The Divine attribute of benevolence.

GLOSSARY

Chochmah — (lit. wisdom); The stage of the intellectual process for abstract conception.

Daas — (lit. knowledge); The third stage of the intellectual process at which concepts, having proceeded from seminal intuition through meditative gestation, now mature into their corresponding dispositions or attributes of character.

Dinim — Divine judgments.

Dveikus — (lit. clinging); A profound concentration and spiritual attachment.

Gadlus — (lit. greatness); The expanded state of consciousness and existence.

Gevurah — (lit. might); The attribute of restraint, associated with the restriction of Divine emanation.

Hod — (lit. splendor); One of the Divine attributes.

Kabbalah — (lit. received tradition); The body of Jewish mystical teachings.

Katnus — (lit. smallness); The constricted and narrow state of consciousness and existence.

Kedusha — (lit. holiness); A passage in the public prayer service with portions recited responsively by the chazan and congregation.

Kelipos — (lit. shells); The outer coverings which conceal Divinity within all creation; hence, the unholy side of the universe.

Kriyas Shema — The recitation of the daily declaration of faith, recited in the morning and evening prayers, as well as before retiring to sleep.

Machzor — The prayer book used specifically for the High Holidays.

Malchus — (lit. kingship); The Divine attribute of might or power.

Midos — Divine and mortal attributes of character, spiritual emotions, and mental states.

Minyan — (lit. number); The quorum of ten necessary for communal prayer.

Mitzvah — (lit. commandment); One of the 613 commandments found in the Torah; a generally good deed.

Mochin — (lit. brains); The three attributes or stages of the intellectual process.

Moshiach — (lit. the anointed one); The Messiah.

Ne'ilah — (lit. closing); The fifth and final prayer service recited on Yom Kippur.

Netzach — (lit. victory); The Divine attribute of eternity.

GLOSSARY

Nitzutzos — sparks.

Penimiyus — (lit. innerness); The endeavor to make one's deeds and attainments an integral part of one's being; the opposite of superficiality.

Pesukei D'Zimrah — (lit. verses of praise); The selection of passages which appear early in the morning prayer service and lead into the declaration of faith.

Ramban — Rabbi Moshe ben Nachman, also known as Nachmanides (1194-1270).

Rosh Hashanah — (lit. head of the year); The solemn New Year holiday.

Satan — The Accusing Angel.

Sefirah — One of the Divine attributes or emanations which are the source of the corresponding faculties of the soul.

Shabbos — (lit. rest); The Sabbath, the Divinely-ordained day of rest on the seventh day of the week.

Shamash — (lit. attendant); The synagogue beadle.

Shechinah — The Divine Presence.

Shefah — The flow of Divine life-force into creation.

Shema — The daily declaration of faith recited in the morning and evening prayers, as well as before retiring to sleep.

Shochet — (lit. ritual slaughterer); One who slaughters and inspects cattle and fowl in the ritually prescribed manner for kosher consumption

Tiferes — (lit. beauty); The Divine attribute of compassion.

Tzaddik — A wholly righteous person (pl. Tzaddikim).

Yesod — (lit. foundation); One of the Divine attributes.

Yetzirah — (lit. formation); The realm of spiritual existence in which the limited nature of the created beings takes on form and definition.

Yom Kippur — The Day of Attonement.

Zeir Anpin — (lit. "small countenance,) The collection of Divine attributes excluding Malchus (might).

BIBLIOGRAPHY

1. BAAL SHEM TOV FAITH LOVE AND JOY Vol. I
   by Tzvi Meir Cohn
2. BAAL SHEM TOV DIVINE LIGHT Vol. II
   by Tzvi Meir Cohn
3. BAAL SHEM TOV HEART OF PRAYER DIVINE LIGHT Vol. III
   by Tzvi Meir Cohn
4. IN PRAISE OF THE BAAL SHEM TOV
   Translated and edited by Dan Ben Amos and Jerome R. Mintz
5. THE PATH OF THE BAAL SHEM TOV
   by Rabbi David Sears
6. ESSENTIAL PAPERS ON CHASSIDISM
   Edited by Gershon David Hundert
7. THE LIGHT BEYOND
   by Rabbi Aryeh Kaplan

8. TZAVA'AT HARIVASH

   by Rabbi Jacob Immanuel Schochet

9. THE LIGHT AND FIRE OF THE BAAL SHEM TOV

   by Maggid Yitzhak Buxbaum

10. THE BESHT

    by Professor Emanuel Etkes

11. THE GREAT MISSION

    by Rabbi Eli Friedman

12. CHASSIDIC MASTERS

    by Rabbi Aryeh Kaplan

13. THE RELIGIOUS THOUGHT OF CHASSIDIM

    by Rabbi Norman Lamm

14. CHASSIDIC MASTERS

    by Rabbi Aryeh Kaplan

15. THE RELIGIOUS THOUGHT OF CHASSIDIM

    by Rabbi Norman Lamm

WWW.MEZUZAH.NET

Home of the World Wide Mezuzah Campaign

The fundamental goal of The World Wide Mezuzah Campaign is to unify the Jewish people. By fulfilling the mitzvah of Mezuzah, this unity can be accomplished by each Jewish person: man, woman or child. The mitzvah can be easily fulfilled by affixing a Mezuzah on the "Doorpost of Your House or upon Your Gates," as required by Jewish law.

Purchase Mezuzahs written in Israel by a Certified Scribe, then checked by a computer for accuracy and finally checked by a second Certified Scribe before we send it to you. Our Mezuzahs are of a very high quality, and they are beautifully written. They are shipped to you in a Mezuzah case ready to mount on your door.

www.mezuzah.net
The World Wide Mezuzah Campaign
A project of the Baal Shem Tov Foundation
A 501(c) (3), nonprofit organization

Baal Shem Tov Times

Spreading the light of the legendary Kabbalah Master and Mystic
Rabbi Yisrael Baal Shem Tov

-A weekly email publication-

Regular Features:

Baal Shem Tov Story
Torah Baal Shem Tov
Heart of Prayer
Divine Light
Kesser Shem Tov

Subscribe to receive your FREE weekly e-mail edition at
www.baalshemtov.com

ABOUT THE AUTHOR

Rabbi Eliezer Shore was born in New York City in 1959, in a secular, Jewish home. He grew up in Great Neck, NY, and attended Sarah Lawrence College from 1977 until 1982. He majored in religious studies, particularly focusing on the religions of the Far East, and minored in music and the performing arts. In 1980, he left college to engage in an intense spiritual search, which took him to England and Scotland, over mountains and into Zen monasteries, and eventually, to a small cabin in the Blue Ridge Mountains of North Carolina. His desire for spirituality continued on returning to college and afterward, as he practiced meditation, martial arts and wilderness survival. In 1982, he met Rabbi Dovid Din, a Kabbalist, hasidic master, and one of the early pioneers in the teshuvah movement. Eliezer became one of R. Din's closest students for the next four years, and learned from him a unique approach to Torah and serving G•d.

In 1986, he moved to Jerusalem to study Torah, and has remained there ever since — aside from a two year stay in New York, during which he received an M.A. in Jewish Education from Yeshiva University, graduating with honors.

In 1996, he received Rabbinic Ordination from R. Zalman Nechemia Goldberg, a member of the Jerusalem

Beit Din, and in 2005, he received a Ph.D. in Jewish Philosophy from Bar Ilan University. His doctoral thesis is on the teachings of Rabbi Nachman of Breslov, and the nexus of language, mystical experience and eros found in the writings of this great hasidic master.

He has taught at numerous institutions around Israel. Most notably, Bat Ayin Yeshiva, in Gush Etzion, the Rothberg School at Hebrew University, Jerusalem, the Overseas Program at Bar Ilan University, Michlalah Jerusalem, and the David Cardozo Academy.

He writes on topics of Jewish spirituality, and his articles have appeared in Parabola Magazine, Sh'ma, HaModia, and other publications. From 1991 until 2000, he edited and published Bas Ayin: A Journal of Jewish Spirituality, which was distributed free worldwide. From 1998 until 2001, he edited the Orthodox Union's popular Pardes Project, under the direction of R. Yaacov Haber.

He is also a dynamic storyteller, whose original tales and retellings have appeared in anthologies and have been read over international radio. In 1997, he founded the Jerusalem Storytelling Circle, as well as delivered weekly stories on a local, Jerusalem radio station.

He lives in the Ramat Eshkol neighbourhood of Jerusalem with his wife and children.

For more information go to www.eliezershore.com

Also Published by BST Press

BAAL SHEM TOV FAITH LOVE AND JOY Vol. I

BAAL SHEM TOV DIVINE LIGHT Vol. II

BAAL SHEM TOV HEART OF PRAYER Vol. III

BAAL SHEM TOV GENESIS Vol. I

BAAL SHEM TOV EXODUS Vol. II

BAAL SHEM TOV LEVITICUS Vol. III

BAAL SHEM TOV NUMBERS Vol. IV

BAAL SHEM TOV DEUTERONOMY Vol. V

BAAL SHEM TOV HOLY DAYS Vol. VI

Printed in Great Britain
by Amazon